Death

THE ART OF LIVING SERIES

Series Editor: Mark Vernon

From Plato to Bertrand Russell philosophers have engaged wide audiences on matters of life and death. *The Art of Living* series aims to open up philosophy's riches to a wider public once again. Taking its lead from the concerns of the ancient Greek philosophers, the series asks the question "How should we live?". Authors draw on their own personal reflections to write philosophy that seeks to enrich, stimulate and challenge the reader's thoughts about their own life.

Clothes *John Harvey*
Commitment *Piers Benn*
Death *Todd May*
Deception *Ziyad Marar*
Distraction *Damon Young*
Faith *Theo Hobson*
Fame *Mark Rowlands*
Forgiveness *Eve Garrard and David McNaughton*
Hunger *Raymond Tallis*
Illness *Havi Carel*
Me *Mel Thompson*
Middle Age *Christopher Hamilton*
Money *Eric Lonergan*
Pets *Erica Fudge*
Science *Steve Fuller*
Sport *Colin McGinn*
Wellbeing *Mark Vernon*
Work *Lars Svendsen*

Death

Todd May

ACUMEN

First published in 2009 by Acumen
Reprinted 2010, 2011, 2013

Acumen Publishing Limited
4 Saddler Street
Durham
DH1 3NP
www.acumenpublishing.co.uk

ISBN: 978-1-84465-164-1

British Library Cataloguing-in-Publication Data
A catalogue record for this book is available
from the British Library.

Typeset in Warnock Pro.
Printed in the UK by 4edge Ltd, Essex.

Contents

Acknowledgements   vii

1. Our dealings with death   1

2. Death and immortality   45

3. Living with death   79

Further reading   115
References   117
Index   119

Acknowledgements

I should like to thank the series editor, Mark Vernon, and Steven Gerrard at Acumen for giving me the opportunity to write this book, and Kate Williams for seeing it through the production process. I have often remarked that the philosophical profession spends too much time removed from issues of importance to people who do not do academic philosophy. More recently, I developed the desire to write a book that my kids could draw lessons from as they got older. When I saw *The Art of Living* series appear, I realized that a reflection on the difficult issue of death would be the best way for me to offer those lessons.

There are many people from whom I have drawn my own lessons in thinking about death. None of them, however, has taught me as much as my high school English teacher and cross-country coach, Tek Lin. Although his name is not mentioned in the text, his influence is everywhere across it. Any wisdom that might have found its way into these pages undoubtedly had its source in his words and actions.

This book is dedicated, of course, to my offspring (no longer children): David, Rachel and Joel. It is also dedicated to my wife, Kathleen, who daily offers reasons to continue to live.

1. Our dealings with death

In the spring of 2004 I took a flight from the airport in Greenville, South Carolina to New York's LaGuardia. I was going to visit my step-grandmother, a woman I had become close to over the years. She was dying of cancer, and this would be one of the last chances I would have to see her. I had taken a weekend flight, as I had several times before, in order to have a couple of days to spend with her in her apartment in the Bronx. For several minutes of that flight, however, it was not her death that concerned me, but my own.

The approach to LaGuardia's runway usually goes from east to west. When we fly up from South Carolina, the plane veers right over Brooklyn and Queens, then turns back around to the left towards Manhattan, and makes its descent. From the left side of the plane, where I usually sat, one could see the Manhattan skyline as one turned towards Brooklyn. On this particular day, that is exactly what happened, until we were about to land.

Then the plane began ascending once again, heading towards Manhattan. There was no announcement from the flight deck, but it was clear we were going to midtown. I could see the Empire State Building in front of us, a bit to the left. As we headed towards the Empire State Building, the cabin became very quiet. At first people were asking their neighbours what was happening. Then conversation petered out altogether.

From where I sat, the plane clearly seemed to be heading for the Empire State Building. It was an eerie moment. I remember seeing the building from an odd angle: the top was straight ahead of me. I could see the sky beyond it, and to my left was downtown. I almost felt as though I could look into the windows and see people at work.

In a way, all this angered me. I grew up in New York, and have always loved the Empire State Building. I had never had the same feeling about the Twin Towers, which (I guess this dates me a bit) seemed to me a bit pretentious: the newcomers who lorded it over the more venerable building on 34th Street. This might seem to be an odd thought to have at this moment, but, as people often say, time seemed to slow down.

My thoughts first went into business mode. I recalled that I had told my wife Kathleen where all the important papers were, and tried to remember whether I had them all up to date. I asked myself what my last interaction with each of my three children had been, and was relieved that it was a positive one. I had hugged each of my kids, and told them I was looking forward to seeing them. I noticed that my stomach was in a knot, and that my fingers were cold. I looked out of the window and saw the Empire State Building getting closer. I figured that I was going to die (there was no "we" for me at that moment).

And then I realized something that has never left me. I realized that I had not regretted my life. There had been disappointments. I had lived in South Carolina for many more years than I had planned to, more years than I had wanted to. I hadn't had as much contact with my friends as I would have liked, and had not visited very often this city that I had grown up in and was about to die in. But I also knew, at that moment, that I would not have traded this life I had lived for another one. I would not have worked harder to get a more prestigious job at the expense of being able to spend time with my kids, or have a spontaneous breakfast with my wife here and there, or run a hard Saturday workout that left me spent for the rest of the day. The life I had lived was not the one I would have chosen, if I had been asked at some point early in my studies or my career. But, having lived it, I would not have traded it in for another one.

Of course I didn't die that day. The plane gained enough altitude to pass over the Empire State Building (but not by much, it seemed to me). As it turns out, when we were about to land, a smaller plane decided it would be a neat idea to land at LaGuardia at that same moment, and our pilot had to make a quick move. He was concentrating on navigating us safely through airspace that, since 9/11, had become fraught, so he didn't have time to announce what was happening until after it was over. Although I would have liked to know what was going on, I took this to be an exercise in good judgement on his part. And, in the end, it gave me a chance to reflect on my life in a way and with an urgency that I would probably not otherwise have done.

You'll not be surprised that I have not forgotten that day. At least some of you who read these words will have had an experience like it, when you knew you were going to die but had time to ponder what it all meant. And I have carried lessons from that day. I keep in mind what emerged as important in those seeming last moments, and try to cultivate it. And I try, with more or less success, to keep perspective on the rest.

It might also seem that the fact of death, the fact that I am mortal, turned out to be a good thing on that day. After all, if I were immortal I would neither have had a chance to reflect on my life nor known what it meant to me to have lived this particular life. None of that would have mattered. Whatever mistakes I had made, there would have been all the time in the world to correct them (well, assuming that everyone I cared about was also immortal). And whatever joys I had had, they would have lost a bit of their lustre with my knowing that I might experience those same joys an infinity of times again.

But there is another side to that coin. I might have died. Planes, as we have learned, do crash into buildings. And if I had died – that is to say, if I had not been immortal – I would not have seen my wife or my children again. I would not have felt the righteous lassitude that

3

comes with a hard workout, or the fascination of a new idea garnered from a book of philosophy. Those joys, which meant so much, which gave me the life I realized I did not regret, would be over.

To see both these sides of death is, I believe, to begin to reflect on it. Death is tragic, arbitrary and meaningless. At the same time it can, because of the particular way it is tragic, arbitrary and meaningless, open out on to a fullness of life that would not exist without it. What we shall investigate in this book, looking periodically at what philosophers and writers have said about death, is the role that death plays in our lives, as well as the ways we try to escape its power and what might happen to us or for us if we can face it squarely.

I would like to make a bold claim right here at the outset: the fact that we die is the most important fact about us. There is nothing that has more weight in our lives. This doesn't mean, of course, that there aren't other important facts about us. Human beings love, work, have sex, create friendships, embark on lifelong projects, undergo intense emotions, even watch others die. These are not insignificant. A life without at least some of these things would probably not be one worth living, at least to the person living it. (Maybe it would have been worth living in the eyes of others, for example, one's parents.) For most of us, there is not one particular fact about us that is the *only* important fact. Death, too, is not the only important fact about us. But it is the *most* important one.

Why is this? Because it is the end of every other fact about us. It is the end of our friendships, our projects, every one of our involvements in the world. Although death is not the only important fact about us, it has the capacity, in a way no other aspect of us does, to absorb every other fact, to bring every other aspect of our lives under its sway.

One might say that a great love will do the same thing. A love that becomes the focus of one's life seems to centre the world on the person loved. What matters is only to be with the beloved. Nothing else seems of account. The joy or sadness of one's own life seems to hinge on small gestures of the one loved; a smile or an arched eyebrow take on outsized significance. And one's own ultimate happiness is hitched to the happiness of the other. Many of us have at least had moments like this: small periods of great love. It is difficult to sustain such a love over a lifetime. But even if it could be done, even if it has been done, it is still not as absorbing as death.

Even when love is at its peak, we still eat. And we can enjoy the taste of food. It may taste better in the presence of the beloved, but its taste will, at least sometimes, not go unnoticed. We will read the newspapers, or at least check out the news on the internet. There will be events we will read about that move us one way or another. A war, a massacre, starvation: even in love, we are not immune to revulsion at these things. Even small joys, such as one's sports team winning a game, register a tick on one's emotional Geiger counter. (Except perhaps for fans, like me, of the New York Knicks, who wait in vain for such ticks.)

Nothing like this happens with death. Nothing escapes it. It encompasses us without remainder. And not only does it encompass us, bringing everything about us within its vortex, but it then negates everything it encompasses. A great love can make us see different aspects of our world through the lens of that love. The world remains there for us, but it looks different in all of its aspects from what it would look like otherwise. In death, the world is no longer there. It doesn't look different. It disappears.

I taught a seminar on death once, to a group of upper-level undergraduate students. The first day I asked them to put their books aside and take out a piece of paper and a pencil. Then I asked them to write four or five of the most important things in their lives on the piece of paper, and fold it up. I promised them that nobody would see what they had written. When they were done, I asked them to pass the papers to me, folded over so that they couldn't be seen. I assured them that I wasn't interested in what they had written. What mattered was that each of them knew what he or she had on the paper, that what each of them had written was before their minds. When they had all passed the papers to me, I gathered them in a small pile. I asked them to focus on the paper, and on what they had written. Then I took the pile and slowly tore it into little shreds. That, I told them, is what each of them – each of us – needed to confront. That is what we had to understand, as best we could.

That is what makes death the most important fact about us: its ability to negate every other element of our lives. And there is more. There is another aspect of death, one that we will revisit later but is worth bringing into discussion now, in order to see death's ongoing significance in our lives. To see it, let's start with a counterfactual example. Let's suppose, contrary to the way things really are, that death was something of which we were unaware until it happened. It would be as though death were a bolt from the blue. We lived our lives, engaged in our various commitments and involvements, and then one day we just stopped living. It's a difficult world to imagine, since we would have to account for how we notice other people no longer living without our wondering what that might have to do with us. But let's suppose we could do it. Would that change anything about the role death plays in our lives? If we had no awareness of it, would it remain the most important fact about us?

It would still, to be sure, be the negation of our world. But it would seem to play less of a role in our ongoing lives. We would die, but the fact that we were going to die would not have a hold on us. We would not be gripped by it. We would go about our lives as though we would live forever, or at least not considering that we wouldn't, since, with death out of the picture, we would also probably not think much about living forever. It would just be natural. We would be living, and that would be that. Until, of course, it stopped.

But, of course, things aren't like that. We are not unaware of death. It is always there, with us. It may not be present to little children, but it surely is present to grownups. My oldest son recently learned to drive, and my wife and I have done our level best to instil the fact of death into his consciousness. As we grow older, see people disappear from our lives or face situations where we fear our own lives are at stake, the recognition of death is always there. This is not to say that we always meditate on it. In fact, and we'll return to this soon, we usually try to escape thinking about it. Even in escaping it, however, it is with us. It is with us *because* we are trying to escape it.

It may be that humans are the only animals with an ongoing sense of their own death. I don't know. Surely, many animals have some awareness of their death, especially when it seems imminent. Animals will cower in fear, or lash out aggressively. Keeping oneself alive seems to be a mandate in the animal world, one that is wired in (which is not to say that there aren't individual animals – human and otherwise – that lose the will to live. But these are the exceptional cases). To seek to remain alive when one's life is threatened, however, is not the same as having an ongoing awareness of one's death. It is more like the counterfactual case I just described, with the addition of an alarm of some kind going off when death is in the neighbourhood.

In order for death to be with us in the way that it is, there has to be more than an awareness of one's demise in the face of a threat. There has to be some higher level awareness. In particular, there needs to be a recognition of one's life as having a trajectory. There is a beginning, an end and the period in between. There also has to be, and we will revisit this point many times, a recognition that death could happen at any time. One is mortal, not only at the end of one's life, but all throughout it. Without the awareness of the trajectory of one's life and its ongoing vulnerability to death, death would have a less significant role to play in one's life.

Are there animals that have the capacity for this higher-level conception of their lives and the role that death plays? It seems difficult to say. Given evolutionary history, there are surely intermediate stages between complete unawareness and full human recognition.

How that more or less murky awareness works is difficult to sort out. But that humans, with our advanced capacity for memory, reflection and projection into the future, that we are attached at every moment to the fact of our death cannot be denied. We can seek to elude it, but it remains with us. As animals who are aware of where our lives are headed, and that we may not get there, our death is always with us.

We humans, then, are the creatures that are characterized, first and foremost, by the fact that we die. I have said that this is the most important fact about us. But some may want to deny this. They may want to say that we are talking at too abstract a level. By the term *abstract* here, I don't mean difficult or complicated. I mean instead abstracted from the specifics of people's lives. It may be easy to argue, at the level of generality we're talking at here, that death is the most important fact about us. But it could well be that death, while in some sense the most important fact about human beings, is not necessarily the most important fact about *each* of us. It could be that there are particular lives that have more important facts about them than that they are going to die. It could even be that many particular lives are that way.

Here's an example. A family undergoes the death of a child. It happens a lot, particularly in places where there aren't enough resources to keep the population going. Let's imagine the case in a little more detail. A child has a debilitating disease, one that resists medical treatment. His or her health slowly disintegrates in front of the family's eyes. They have to endure this. The parents, in particular, have to watch helplessly as their child moves inevitably towards death. Wouldn't this fact be as important, more important, to the lives of the parents than their own dying? Wouldn't their own deaths pale in comparison?

In coming to terms with this example, we cannot take the easy way out. We cannot say that this example also involves death, so it has some similarity to the issue of death as we are posing it. It doesn't.

As we have been speaking of death, it is not the death of someone else that is the fundamental fact of one's life. It is one's own death. As the philosopher Martin Heidegger reminds us, the salient fact about death is that it is for each of us *my own* death. We can hear about the death of others, go to funerals, even see someone die. These are weighty matters. However, they do not replace the singularity of one's own death. It is not that one's own death matters more in the grand scheme of things than the death of someone else. It is that one's own death cannot be understood by coming to terms with someone else's death. The silencing of one's experience, including the experience of the silencing of another's experience, remains intimately one's own in a way that cannot be understood by analogy with anyone or anything else.

This returns us to the question then of how to think about the death of one's child. I have said that death is the most important fact about us as humans. Couldn't it be, though, that some traumatic event – or perhaps some glorious event, although this would be harder to imagine – would be more important to a particular life than the fact of one's own death? Could it be that in light of this traumatic event, death loses its power? The end of our experience, then, becomes something less to be dreaded, and maybe even welcomed.

There are two responses to be given to an example like this. The first is easier and more straightforwardly philosophical. It may seem like a way of dodging the example, but it reminds us of something central to who we are. This response is to say that death is the most important fact about us *as human beings*. As particular humans, our individual trajectories may differ. Some of us have difficult lives that may not even appear to us to be worth living. (In 1988, I met someone in a refugee camp in the Gaza Strip. He was seventeen. He told me that he had confronted his father once, demanding to know why he would bring him into such a world.) For others of us, I suspect most, the difficulties of life do not override its meaningfulness. But what we, as human beings, have in common is a death whose inevitability is coupled with uncertainty: a death that will end our experience and can do so at any time. Moreover, this inevitability and this uncertainty are aspects of death that we cannot escape; we are, ultimately, creatures who are aware of the end that awaits us. And finally, that awareness structures the way we go about our lives, even – perhaps especially – when we act as though we were never going to die.

Even if this is right, it doesn't seem to answer the question of whether in cases like our example death is a more important fact in particular lives than some other event or fact about those lives. In order to address that question more directly, I want to distinguish two different questions. These questions are both centred on the importance of facts about one's life, but unfold in two different ways. The first question is: what makes a life meaningful or worthwhile, or on the contrary saps life of meaning? The second question is: what is the most important fact about a life, the one that structures it more than any other? The importance of traumatic events lies in their role in addressing the first question. The importance of death has to do with the second.

Things can happen, good or bad, that lend life meaning or that steal it away. When each of us looks back on our lives, he or she will ask about those things. They will involve projects we have undertaken, relationships we have cultivated and events that have occurred. For some of us, one hopes very few, among those events will be the death of a child. That death will be a defining event for the life that has had to face it. It will make that life seem less worthwhile to the one who has lived it. It will be part of the content of one's life that will probably be reflected on as one asks about the meaningfulness of that life.

The importance of death lies elsewhere. It lies not in the content of one's life, in one's personal trajectory. Rather, it lies in the way it structures how we go about our lives. And it does so in a way that is perhaps more important than any other fact about us. We live life always in the shadow of the fact that we will die. What we do, how we do it, the attitude we take towards it, happens against the background knowledge that each of us is mortal. Once again, this does not mean that everything in a life is reducible to death. There are many important facts about human lives. Rather, it means that, among those important facts, our mortality holds a special place.

It even structures the relation to a child's death. The meaningfulness of a parent's life is, as for all humans, the meaningfulness of a mortal life. The parent will reflect on the child's life and death and the place it has in his or her life from the perspective of someone who will themselves die. Everything would be different, as we shall see in the next chapter, if the parent were immortal. But parents are not immortal, and their approach to the child's death will be structured by that fact.

We might put the point this way. There are projects, relationships and events that are the *whats* of every life. Death is one of those *whats*, but its operation is as a *how*. When it becomes a *what*, when it happens, there are no more *hows* to a life. But before it happens it operates on life as a *how*: the most important *how* of which a human life is composed.

I have offered a few reasons to think that death is the most important fact about us, and have tried to show, at least initially, the way in which it is important. The evidence for death's central place in life is everywhere around us. In order to see it, let's take as an example an arena of life that is centrally important for much of the world's population: religion. Among the roles of religion is to deal with death. It is an important role. And the way most religions deal with death is by offering the solace of a way to continue life. For me, one of the urgent aspects of thinking about death is that I don't believe in an afterlife. Therefore, I need to come to grips with my life in its brevity and its finality (a finality that was particularly clear to me on the plane that day in 2004). Most religions recognize that people face death, and they recognize that understanding or somehow coming to terms with it is of central importance to people. However, rather than confronting death as an end, a number of religious traditions think of death differently, as something other than an end.

Religious traditions and death

Of course, most religions don't claim we don't die. But there is, for many religions, a particular sense in which we don't really die: we don't die in the sense that there is no more of us after we are dead. In order to see how this works, and how death is central to many traditions of religious experience, let's take a couple of examples. In taking these examples, we should at once recognize that religious traditions are rich and varied. The reasons I have chosen the examples I have is that they represent common approaches to particular religious traditions. Many people will recognize themselves in them, although others of the same faith will not.

The obvious place to look is at the monotheistic religious tradition. Take a standard view of Christianity. When you die, you are assigned to heaven or hell (or in some cases purgatory) based on the life you've lived. Not all of you arrives at one of these destinations. Your body is left behind. It is your soul that faces judgement, and therefore the result of that judgement. It is sent to one place or another, depending on how it has conducted itself during your earthly existence. That is what is meant by an afterlife.

I want to call attention to one particular aspect of this story. In having an afterlife, you survive your own death. It's not just the survival that is the point here. It's also that it is *you* that survives it. The *you* that exists after you die is in some sense the same *you* that existed during your life. Logically, it must be. Otherwise, the judgement on your soul would be pointless. Why would somebody other than you be judged for what you did? No, it is you who is judged, and you who is consigned to heaven or hell.

This also means that the you who is consigned must be the same you who is judged. Again, it wouldn't make any sense to judge someone and then give the reward or punishment for that judgement to someone else, or to create someone else to be the recipient of it. If that happened it wouldn't really be a reward or punishment. It would be like a judge passing a sentence on a criminal and then sending someone else to jail, or making up somebody to send to jail. The point of rewards and punishments is precisely that they are meted out to the person who has earned them. If we think of heaven and hell as reward and punishment respectively – and it's hard to imagine how else we are to think of them – then they must be assigned to those who have been judged deserving of them.

The upshot of this is that there is a continuity between three stages of your existence. The first stage is your existence here on this earth, your life in the mundane sense. The second is your existence after you die but before you are judged. The third is your existence after you are judged. These three stages, in order for the common Christian doctrine of the afterlife to make sense, must all be stages of *your* existence. It must be you at every point in this process. It doesn't have to be all of you; your body doesn't stay with you in the last two stages. But it must be the core of you, the essence of who you are. That's what your soul is: the essence of who you are. In the Christian tradition, your body is mostly a vehicle for your soul (although it does have particular weaknesses toward sin to which a bodiless soul would not be subject).

The fact that it is you who remains in these three stages is, of course, both the promise and fear associated with the Christian afterlife. The possibility that you will exist in eternal bliss is a source of hope only if it is you who will do so. By the same token, eternal damnation is not a source of threat (or a motivation to act well) unless it is you who will be facing the torments. But there is something else, something beneath the promise and fear, that is, I believe, a source of comfort in the afterlife in this conception of it.

That something else is simply your continuity. Whether you spend your eternity in heaven or hell, whether you are blessed or damned, you will still exist. You – the essence of you – will not die. There will be no total negation of your experience in the way we described a few pages ago.

One might ask, and it is a good question: what of your experience will remain? Will all your memories survive in the latter two stages? This seems unlikely, since many of them don't even survive during the first stage. But something of your memories must survive, in order for you to remain who you are. It's hard to imagine how it could be you who is judged if there is no past you carry with you. In addition, what aspects of your way of being will remain after your corporeal death? It's hard to say, although, as with memories, there must be enough of them – or at least the most important aspects – to make you who you are. Something of your intellect must survive, your emotional orientation, your interpersonal style must be subject to judgement and to the results of that judgement. What the specifics are may be hard to say, but one thing is certain. Whatever it is of your experience that survives, it must lie at your core. It must be deeply a matter of who you are.

And that is the source of comfort a conception of the afterlife brings. One may fear the ceaseless agony of an eternal afterlife in hell, but one is at least assured that there will be a life: one's own life, the core of who one is. One's joys may end, but one's life will not. And so a conception of the afterlife brings with it some comfort, no matter how fearsome its consequences may be. There are also, of course, mechanisms in most Christian denominations to allow one to avoid the worst-case scenario. But even on that scenario, one thing will not be lost: oneself. The thing that death threatens to take away will remain more or less intact.

When we see this, we also see how central this idea of the integrity of oneself after death is to this common experience of Christianity. Without this conception of the afterlife, one that retains each individual soul, Christianity would become a very different religion from the one that it is. (Once again, not all Christian denominations require the belief in an afterlife, although that is the usual approach. Others, many of whom take the New Testament in a more literary sense, interpret discussions of an afterlife more metaphorically.) However, it is not only Christianity that keeps death at bay in this particular way. Much of Judaism and Islam do as well. Moreover, so do Eastern religions.

Buddhism, the most popular of Eastern religions, is a case in point. Buddhism emphasizes the withdrawal of attachment from things of this world. It seeks the extirpation of desire. Desire is what leads to suffering, both of oneself and of others. Human beings desire things: material success, recognition, comfort, love and so on. The problem is that no amount of any of these things will slake desire. Desire just transfers its want to something else or something more. By allowing ourselves to be subject to our desire, we are eternally unsatisfied. We can never be at peace as long as we desire. We will always suffer.

Desire leads not only to our suffering but to the suffering of others as well. It is through desire that we compete with others, that we want what they have, that we compare ourselves to them and, ultimately, that we are willing to harm them. Without desire, one would have no reason to treat others badly.

However, desire is difficult to extinguish. As a result, many of us wind up suffering and bringing suffering to others. This is where the doctrine of karma becomes important. I should note here that there are different ways to interpret the doctrine of karma. One way, although it is much less popular, is to interpret it as the unending carousel of desire that one must step off in order to achieve peace. On this interpretation, the Buddhist "wheel of samsara" refers to the unending slaking and return of desire. One desires, has that desire met or not met, and then moves on to the next desire, always unsatisfied. This way of interpreting karma does not engage the issue of death. The other interpretation of karma is the one most people are familiar with. It requires reincarnation.

On this interpretation, the wheel of samsara refers to cycles of life and rebirth that one undergoes until one achieves nirvana, that is, an existence void of desire. Roughly, the idea is this. To the extent that one is directed by desire, one will suffer and bring suffering to others. When one dies, one is reborn in a higher or lower form, depending on how much one has allowed one's life to be so directed. Less desire allows one to be reborn into a higher life; more desire directs one downward. Karma refers to what one has done in one's life. It is not merely descriptive though. It has a normative status. We could say that one's karma is both the sum total of a particular life and the grade that life has earned on the scale of eliminating desire and its effects. Thus one's karma situates one relative to the next life.

The question for us is: what is it that is reborn? As with the type of Christianity we discussed above, your body does not stay with you after death. When you're reborn, it is into a different body. It is your mind or your soul – again as in Christianity – that is reborn. If your karma consists in what you have made of yourself in a particular life, your rebirth situates you in a particular karmic state in your next one.

Your karmic state is not your fate. If it were, everyone would be reborn as the same thing he or she was in a previous life. In Buddhism, one chooses to work on oneself, or chooses not to. That determines how one will be reborn, at least until one achieves nirvana, when one will not be reborn at all. At that point, one steps off the wheel of samsara. So who you are evolves either upward or downward, depending on how you go about your life.

This is in contrast to Christianity. In Christianity, as in Judaism and Islam, you have only one temporal life. The judgement on your soul happens once. In Buddhism (as in Hinduism), each life is judged, depositing you in the next life in a form that matches the karma of your previous one. We might put things this way. In the Judeo-Christian tradition, earthly life is a test for the afterlife. In Buddhism, earthly life is a problem to be overcome. While in the Judeo-Christian tradition the desire associated with temporal life must be mastered in order to be worthy of heaven, in Buddhism the desire associated with temporal life must be mastered in order to avoid more temporal life. For Buddhists, life is suffering. Overcoming life is then the goal.

Does this mean that the Buddhist relation to death as an end is different from the Christian one we discussed earlier? In one way, there is something more dynamic about the Buddhist conception of who one is in relation to death. While for Christians, there is only one earthly death, for Buddhists there are many. And who one is in the face of a particular death may be different from who one was in the face of an earlier death, and who one might be when confronted with a future death. In Christianity, there is a strict continuity between the you who lives on earth, the you who is judged, and the you who follows that judgement. Buddhists, however, see the possibility of developing different yous, with different karma, in each life. Does this alter the essential question of whether you survive your death?

The answer here is no. The dynamism of Buddhist reincarnation still involves a you that survives each death. Over the course of your lives, you change. You develop yourself, or fail to do so. What remains steady across lives is precisely this evolution. But evolution requires a continuity. And continuity requires a you that is continuous. In that sense, although you change over time and lives, it is always you that survives each death and is reincarnated in the next one.

One might ask about whether, when you have achieved nirvana, you continue to exist. Since you have stepped off the wheel of samsara, you have stopped evolving. Is there still a you there? This is a difficult question to answer. One might say that a you remains.

The you that remains is a you that is at peace, one that has exited the turbulence of this world. It is a perfect you, but a you nonetheless. On the other hand, one could say that that you only lasts until your death, and then it disappears, since there is nothing to reincarnate.

There are those who study Buddhism who will want to take issue with the interpretation I have offered here. After all, they point out, for Buddhism the self is a myth. There is no self, only the ever-changing process of the cosmos. This is true. All Buddhist doctrine denies the idea of a distinct self. The significance of this denial, though, depends on one's interpretation of Buddhism. For those who do not embrace the doctrine of reincarnation, it is easy to see how there is no self. As we shall see much later with Taoism, one is like a wave on the ocean. There is no distinct self; only a temporary fold of the cosmos that one calls oneself.

Things are more complicated with the doctrine of reincarnation, however. If, in a way, the self is an illusion, in another way it is not. As with the Christian doctrine we discussed, there must be something that survives death in order to get reincarnated. And that something must be continuous with the previous life, or else the nature of one's reincarnation would be entirely arbitrary. We might put the point this way: the self is an illusion that only dissipates when one achieves nirvana.

The core analogy between Buddhism and Christianity as we have discussed them here could be put this way. In Christianity, one changes over the course of one's life. In Buddhism, one changes over the course of one's life and over the course of one's lives. In both cases, however, there is a recognizable someone – a you – that does the changing. And, which is crucial for our reflection here, that you survives death, either once or many times. You don't cease to exist. And so you, the essence of you, doesn't really die. In Eastern religions, as with the monotheistic tradition, death is ultimately something that is avoided. It's not just that it can be avoided.

It is essentially avoided. If we can put it this way, it is unavoidably avoided. Whatever happens to your body (or your bodies), you continue to exist.

What does this tell us? Why does it matter that in these major religious traditions of the world, one necessarily survives one's own death? It gives us a clue as to the significance, and dread, of death in human life. If, as the cliché goes, there are no atheists in foxholes, it is because one of the important roles of religion in life is to master the fear of death. This is not, of course, the only role of religion. There are roles of cosmic explanation, of moral guidance, of community membership. Moreover, I am not taking a stand here on the truth of any particular religion. For the record, I am an atheist (which is why I don't believe in an afterlife). But, on the other hand, I have never been in a foxhole. My point is not to pronounce on the veracity of any or all religions, but rather to call attention to the importance of surviving death that characterizes these major religious traditions. And my point in doing so is to show how important a theme death is in thinking about the shape and status of our lives.

The reason for appealing to the religious tradition is that, for much of the world's population, religion provides the conceptual framework for thinking about one's life. It is through religion that most people ask the ultimate questions about who they are and where they stand in the larger scheme of things. Therefore, the religious approach to death expresses the aspirations people have in regard to their own death. The fact that common approaches to religions are committed to people's surviving their own death tells us both that death is a central theme of life and that it haunts life to the extent that we hope to avoid its finality. Perhaps this is not true for all of us, but it holds for the overwhelming majority – even atheists.

In this book, we will confront death in its finality. The underlying assumption is that one does not survive one's death. In this sense, we will not appeal to the religious tradition we have just surveyed

19

in order to understand and deal with death. This might raise a question for our project. Many readers of this book are likely to be religious or at least to be open to the possibility of religious truth. Does the approach we take here create an obstacle for thinking about death? Does it make the themes we consider here irrelevant for such readers?

I don't think so. When I taught my seminar on death, we operated under the same assumption. I had several students in the course who told me they were religious and believed in an afterlife. They said they were interested in the themes of the course, however, since their faith did not preclude doubt. The course confronted those doubts directly. Even for those who are religious, then, it doesn't seem worthless to reflect on death as a finality rather than as a stage in one's existence. Faith can exist alongside doubt. In that vein, this book might be seen as an attempt to rigorously follow where doubt about an afterlife might lead. Moreover, religious traditions are broad and varied. Even those who believe in some kind of afterlife can have divergent views of how it works and what aspects of oneself may or may not survive one's death. The views we have canvassed here are mainstream ones, but there are plenty of individual variations in the content of faith. (I recall once seeing a church in Rome, Santa Maria dell'Orazione e Morte [St Mary of Prayer and Death], that had death-heads on the doorway and skeletons and themes of death throughout. If any structure was going to put one in confrontation with death, this was it.)

How about the person who is confident of an afterlife, so confident that doubt does not enter in? He or she is certain of one of the doctrines we have just reviewed, or of something like it. Death, for this person, elicits no anxiety. The only question for this person is whether he or she is worthy of a good afterlife. For this person, I must admit, the following reflections have little to offer. If death really isn't the end of one's existence, then coming to terms with it as though it were is an empty intellectual exercise. I don't suspect, however, that there are many people who fit this description. On the one hand, for many professed atheists, Blaise Pascal's wager remains a good bet. (Pascal was a French philosopher who wrote that one should act as though God exists, since there is nothing lost in doing so if God does not exist but plenty lost in *not* doing so if God does exist.) Just so, I suspect that most religious people are not so certain of their faith that it would be pointless to ask about death as though there were no afterlife.

What is death?

If we are to think rigorously about death as a finality, then, we should perhaps take some time to ask what death is or, better, what it is to be a being that dies. We have touched on this question in our reflections up until now, asking about the importance of death in life. However, it would be worth coming up with a systematic overview — or at least as systematic as we can make it — of what it is to be a mortal creature and, moreover, a creature that is aware of one's mortality. There have been a number of reflections on human mortality in philosophy. Perhaps, though, none has been so systematic as that of Heidegger in the first chapter of the Second Division of his monumental work *Being and Time*. *Being and Time* is one of the most influential books in the history of philosophy. First published in 1927, it is Heidegger's early magnum opus on what he calls the question of Being or the meaning of Being. In the course of asking this question, he seeks to know the being of the one who asks the question of Being: that is to say, who we are. In Heidegger's view, we are askers of the question of Being. While the reasons he believes this are wide of our purposes, the fact that we askers of the question of Being are mortal is not. Heidegger opens the second division of *Being and Time* with a reflection on what it is for human beings to be mortal.

21

The vocabulary Heidegger uses – and largely invents – in his philosophical work is elusive. The American philosopher John Dewey reportedly said of *Being and Time* that it was just a version of his own *Experience and Nature*, except in "high-falutin' German". However, the themes he isolates and discusses are trenchant. Moreover, they can be rendered in more everyday language. I would like to borrow several of those themes in order to give an overview of the meaning of being a mortal creature that recognizes its mortality. I won't always present these themes exactly as Heidegger has, but anyone familiar with his writing will recognize his hand at work.

In particular, we should look at four themes. First, death is the end of us and of our experience. Secondly, that end is not an accomplishment or a goal; it is simply a stoppage. Thirdly, death is at once inevitable and uncertain. We are certain to die, but we don't know when. So death does not only lie at the end of our lives but in fact pervades them. And, finally, these three characteristics make us wonder whether there is any meaning to our lives.

That death is the end of us and of our experience is precisely what the religious traditions we have canvassed here seek to avoid. In death, we are no longer. This, I must admit, is difficult to imagine. When I think about my death, I often do so by thinking about the world going on after me. But that comes from a perspective that still has me in the picture. It's as though I'm gazing at the world from above or outside it. Everything goes on as before, except that I'm watching it from a box seat. I'm separate from the world, but I'm still there.

The silence that is death, my not being there any longer, is something else again. It seems to resist thought. It is a wall my mind runs up against without being able to penetrate or find its way around. It confronts me, not as a threat to my being (things are already too late for that), but as an incomprehensibility that nevertheless is who I am to become.

For some philosophers, this is the good news about death. The ancient Greek philosopher Epicurus wrote, "Death is nothing to us. For what has been dissolved has no sense-experience, and what has no sense-experience is nothing to us" ("Principal Doctrines", II). It is a pithy analysis of death, one worth lingering over for a moment.

For Epicurus, life is a matter of pleasure and pain. From this is derived the term epicurean, referring to people who dedicate themselves to experiencing all kinds of pleasures. Unfortunately, epicureans follow a philosophy opposite to that of Epicurus himself. Epicurus's view is not that people should seek pleasure, but rather that they should avoid pain. The attempt to seek pleasure is, in fact, self-defeating. It often ends in frustration and, as the Buddhists also understand, desire tends to multiply itself so that it is ultimately unsatisfying. Epicurus' cure for this, however, is distinct from that of the Buddhists. Rather than eliminating desire, one should seek only simple pleasures. A nourishing meal, a place to sleep, friendship and camaraderie: these are the stuff of a good life. When one realizes that nothing more is needed than this, then one will arrive at peace and, for the most part, eliminate pain.

We say "for the most part" here because the view Epicurus commends is still exposed to the vagaries of the world. When Buddhists seek to eliminate desire, it is to make us entirely invulnerable to what happens around us. Someone without desire cannot be affected by anything that happens to him or to her. By contrast, someone who still has certain needs, even simple ones, is subject to have those needs go unmet. There may be no food available; for large parts of the world's population it is indeed a struggle to find daily nourishment. Friends may be difficult to come by. Here in the US, where competition reigns supreme, it can be hard to discern the friend from the temporary ally. It is true that the simpler one's desires, the less likely they are to be frustrated. But Epicurus does not leave us impregnable to frustration. Nor does he mean to.

Instead, he means to offer us a way of living that is as satisfying as it can be within the natural limits of a human being.

One of those limits concerns death. When it comes to death, he tells us, "all men live in a city without walls" ("Vatican Sayings", 31). How, then, can we confront death without succumbing to the fear it inspires in us? By recognizing that death is nothing to us. When we die, we are no longer. There is nothing left to experience the pain of death. While we are alive, we are capable of experiencing pleasure and pain. But when we die, we are no longer capable of experience. We either are, or we are not. If we are, there is no death, and so nothing to fear from it. If we are not, then we have already died, and there is nothing left to be able to fear from it.

This may strike us as a way of avoiding the confrontation with death. But it should be noticed that if it is, it comes from entirely the opposite direction from that of the religious traditions we considered above. For those traditions, the overcoming of the fear of death is rooted in our surviving our own death. Epicurus, by contrast, finds consolation precisely in the fact that we don't survive it. For him, it is our utter elimination that vitiates death as a source of pain. There can be no pain if there is nobody there to experience it.

One might want to object here that in order to take this view of death, one has to take on all of Epicurus's philosophy, and particularly the idea that life is reducible to pleasure and pain. If there is nothing more than pleasure and pain, and death ends all of that, then death is nothing to us. But isn't Epicurus's view just too reductive? Don't our lives involve engagements that are meaningful beyond their being sources of pleasure and pain? In fact, don't we often take on projects that involve pain in order to accomplish things whose significance is not merely a matter of providing pleasure?

We will return to these questions again, particularly when we discuss the ideas that death is not an accomplishment or a goal and that it is both inevitable and uncertain. For the moment, however, I want to defend the idea that his view can be divorced from a commitment to life's being nothing more than pleasures and pains. Epicurus' core thought around death in the passage we're considering here is that to be dead is to be without experience. And to be without experience is to be without suffering. We may fear death from the standpoint of a living being, one that would like to continue living. But from the standpoint of death there is nothing to fear.

In other words, Epicurus is not simply reducing life to pleasure and pain. Instead, he is switching perspectives on death, from a living being who fears death to a dead being without experience of fear or anything else. This does not require a reductive view of living. Life can be much richer than just pleasures and pains. However, whatever it is, it still goes silent with death. The very impenetrability of death that I find so frightening is what Epicurus uses to defuse that fear. He does so not by saying that death involves no more pleasures and pains, but that it involves no more experience of any kind. As such, it cannot be a problem to be dead.

The proper question here, is seems to me, is not whether we must embrace Epicurus's wider philosophy in order to find his view of death compelling. We don't. Rather, the question is whether we can reasonably make this switch of perspectives. Can we step outside the perspective of our own lives enough to see things from the perspective of death? Or, better, is the fact that we are nothing in death enough to tear us from our involvements in and with life? Is death's being the end of our experience a way to relieve us of its threatening character, or does it instead heighten the threat to those involvements?

Here is where the second characteristic of death becomes important for us. Death is not an accomplishment. It is not a goal. It is nothing more than a stoppage of our lives. In order to see what this stoppage consists in, Heidegger offers a couple of contrasts. Death is neither a ripening nor a bringing-to-wholeness of life. To say that death is not a ripening is to contrast it, for instance, with a fruit. When a fruit ripens, we can say that it becomes what it was moving towards. Its ripening is the moment at which it is most characteristically the fruit that it is. An apple, for instance, is ready to be picked, and therefore to spread its seeds, when it ripens. This does not imply that the apple has a goal for itself, or that it is the product of some design. It only means that the apple comes, if you will pardon the term, to fruition at ripening.

Death is not like this. It is not the fullest expression of life. It does not bring a life to what it most characteristically is. If anything, death is the opposite. Rather than expressing a life, it obliterates it. It eliminates rather than fulfilling a life's trajectory. Death cannot be regarded as the highest moment of a life, the moment towards which a life moves in order to be most fully that life. Ripening, then, is an inadequate way to conceive death.

For much the same reason, death does not bring life to a whole. We should be clear here. In one sense, not a particularly interesting one, death does make a life whole. This is the sense in which there is no reminder of a person's life when he or she dies. Death makes life a whole by ensuring that nothing is left over of that life. But when we think of wholeness, this is not what we mean. What we're after is rather a sort of satisfying completion, as in a novel or a play. And here, too, we must be clear. The word *satisfying* can be a bit loaded. For a novel or a play to be satisfying, it does not have to be enjoyable. Rather, the end of a novel allows us to reflect back on its meaning. The end of any work of art (or at least any work of art that unfolds temporally) is important. It is in light of this end that we consider what has happened before. In this sense, the end of a novel or a play or a movie or a poem brings the work to wholeness. It completes it, rather than just ending it. (Of course, there are works of art, particularly more recent ones, that resist just this sort of completion. However, they operate by cutting against the grain of expectation set up by traditional works of art.)

This aspect of death reveals to us a bit about the character of our lives. We all have various relationships and projects. Allow me to use, as an example, my relationship with my wife. When I die (or when she dies), our relationship will not come to completion. It will just stop. It will be over, and over in a way that does not give it any meaning that it did not have before. If one of us dies suddenly, this meaninglessness will be evident to the survivor. Death will have conferred nothing on the relationship. It will only have severed it.

Some people will object here that, in a sense, the relationship is not severed. After all, doesn't the dead one continue to live on in the surviving person? Don't we all feel that we carry other people's lives around in us, through their words or their influence or their outlook on life? If this is true, then doesn't the relationship continue after death? Moreover, doesn't it sometimes happen that right after a person dies, the survivors feel closer to that person than they did before? Isn't there an immediate intimacy that's even more intense than the relationship was when the person was living?

When we say that the dead person continues to live on in the survivor or survivors, though, we don't mean this literally. What we mean instead is that the effects of the person and the relationship linger in the survivors. What each of us carries around from the person who has died is not actually a piece of them but an afterglow – sometimes a permanent one – from their *having lived* among us. This afterglow, particularly in the immediacy of a person's having died, does lend itself a certain intimacy. But, again, the intimacy is not with the person himself or herself. That person has died and is no longer there. The intimacy, like the effects, is instead a sort of shadow that both follows me and emanates from me without having an existence independent of me.

This is not meant to diminish the importance of the lingering effects of, or the sense of intimacy with, someone who has died. It is rather to find its proper place, in my ongoing relation to what has been rather than in a relationship whose boundaries cross over on to the other side of death.

From another angle, one might say that if a death is foreseen, if there is time to deal with it, then the relationship can be brought to some sort of completion. This might seem particularly true if both my wife and I live to an old age. I don't believe this is true. If the death of one of us is foreseen, then we will have time to deal with it. We will try to tie up loose ends, make sure that our feelings for each other are clear, express things that might have remained unexpressed if there were more time. But this does not amount to bringing the relationship to completion. It is, instead, a substitute for a relationship that is about to end. What is characteristic of a relationship like this does not lie in any wholeness it might achieve at the end. It lies in the ongoing relationship itself. The relationship I share with my wife is the time we have and have had together, and how we fill and have filled that time. In that sense, our relationship is not like a novel. It does not have an end that brings its meaning to the fore. It is its own meaning. If one of us dies in a way that can be foreseen, we might confer a certain meaning on it. But that is nothing more than a way to deal with the ending of the relationship itself. It is not a way of completing it.

What is true for relationships – familial, friend and otherwise – is also true for other aspects of our lives, particularly those that unfold over longer periods of time. As we go through our lives, we engage ourselves in a number of ongoing projects: vocational, athletic, interpersonal, political and so on. Some of these projects come to completion not by death but by getting finished. If I die while writing a book, this does not bring the book to completion. What brings the book to completion is finishing the book. If our lives are vital ones, we will continue to be involved in projects throughout them. The ones we are engaged in at the end of our lives will not be completed. They will be ended. They will be like threads that have been cut before being attached or tied anywhere. There is a particular tragedy to the death of young people, in part because they have not had the chance to involve themselves in or see through very many projects. Most of their projects have been little more than dreams. That is what we mean when we say they haven't had a chance to live. But the engagement in projects is not only characteristic of the young. What death accomplishes is to cut off whatever projects a person is participating in at the time.

Is this true for everyone, though? Might it be that there are people for whom life becomes a whole that makes the end "the right time to die"? Certainly, this must be possible, and we shall return to this possibility in the next chapter. But the circumstances that would allow it to happen are unusual. It would have to involve not only the removal of oneself from any projects one might be engaged in (or their completion), but also the successful closure of one's relationships. We are not talking here about people who are depressed, people who have given up on life. For people like that, life does not become a whole. It just ceases to be of interest. We are considering people for whom death might be seen as bringing to closure a meaningful life. The people for whom our considerations are relevant here are those who have had a life they – and probably those around them – would consider one worth living. And now it has come to an end, and death provides the final curtain.

One cannot deny that such lives are possible, and that death could be said to bring them to a whole. But neither can their rarity be denied. How many lives are left that do not cut someone off from a set of engagements or relationships or even hopes? Not many. For the vast majority of us, death accomplishes nothing. It merely stops what we would otherwise have wanted to continue: the projects and engagements of our lives.

This brings us back to our reflections on Epicurus. We saw there that one criticism that could be raised of his view is that it reduces life to matters of pleasure and pain. At that time, I claimed that we do not need to embrace that aspect of Epicurus's thought in order to find his perspective on death to be compelling. The issue, to which we shall return in a moment, is whether one can switch viewpoints from that of life to that of death. For the moment, I want to emphasize that we have just seen one of the reasons we cannot reduce life to pleasures and pains. Pleasures and pains are momentary. They have no significant temporal thickness. Pleasures and pains take place over short periods; they are more like the punctuation marks of a life than the life itself. What characterize a human life are engagements. A human life is largely a series of involvements: with others, with one's studies or one's job, with one's activities or one's hobbies. There is pleasure and pain associated with these engagements, but the engagements themselves are about more than pleasure and pain. The projects of raising a child, becoming good at a sport, participating in a political campaign or keeping a farm going cannot be assessed simply on a scale running from pain to pleasure. They are assessed in terms of their meaningfulness, an assessment that resists measure.

Epicurus might reply to us here that even if human life has to do with its engagements, nevertheless in death those engagements are gone. There is nothing to miss about them, since there is nobody there to do the missing. This would be a fair reply, as far as it goes. But it misses the deeper issue. What this fact about human beings points to has more to do with the question of switching perspectives than of reducing life to pleasure and pain. If our lives are matters of ongoing projects, temporally extended engagements, then it becomes difficult for us to let those lives go. Epicurus talks of life as though it involved an on–off switch. Where there is consciousness, awareness, there is life. When that consciousness goes away, there is death. But the consciousness itself is much more than merely being aware. It is also being involved. And the prospect of losing those involvements is a central part of the pain of knowing one is mortal. While it may be true, as Epicurus has it, that in death there is nothing to regret, we who are alive have plenty to regret at the prospect of our deaths. Not the loss of pleasure, about which Epicurus is surely right; what we have to regret, rather, is the stoppage without closure of those engagements, those projects that are largely what a human life consists in.

Having said this, I want to be careful not to reduce all of the goodness of life merely to its projects. There is something to pleasure and pain that needs to be acknowledged. The philosopher Thomas Nagel writes, in his article simply entitled "Death":

There are elements which, if added to one's experience, make life better; there are other elements which, if added to one's experience, make life worse. But what remains when these are set aside is not merely *neutral*: it is emphatically positive ... The additional positive weight is supplied by experience itself, rather than by any of its contents.   (1979: 2)

We might take these contents to be pleasure and pain. But we might also take these contents to be a person's projects. And if we do, then Nagel's point is that, in the absence of all these projects, there is something about life that is itself a pleasure. There is something about life that makes it worth being there, even when one's projects go awry.

Often, when I get a chance, I take an afternoon nap. I like the nap, but I also like the moment of awakening. Lying on my bed, I can look through my window and see a tree against the background of the sky. I have often lived in places where I could wake up from naps seeing trees framed by the sky. And when I look at this, the green of the leaves against the sky's azure, I sometimes find myself both grateful and wistful. For reasons I don't entirely understand, I sometimes tell myself that I will miss that when I die. What will I miss? The colours themselves, just seeing them. Of course, I won't literally miss these things when I die. Epicurus is right about that. But Nagel is right about something here as well. Lying in bed, seeing the green against blue, is not a project of mine. It isn't part of any engagement. But it is a reason to be alive. While most of what makes life meaningful are our ongoing commitments, we should bear this truth of Nagel's in mind as well, if for no other reason than to keep before us the richness and irreducibility of our lives.

31

These reflections already touch on the third theme concerning death: that it is at once inevitable and uncertain. The inevitability of death is an obvious point. We are mortal creatures, therefore we die. The uncertainty of death is hardly less obvious. Although many of us will live longer than twenty or thirty years, we are all aware that death can happen at any time. Whether through a genetic weakness, a car accident or, as I once thought I was, being on the wrong plane at the wrong time, death is always possible. It would be a mistake to say that death is always equally impending; in fact, that might make it less uncertain. There are times when death is less likely, and times when it is more likely. But there is always the possibility of death. Having been born, as the saying goes, I am always old enough for death.

What gives this theme its force is neither of the two characteristics isolated from each other. It lies rather in their combination. It is both the fact that I cannot escape my death and that I cannot control when that death will be that this third theme points to. If I could escape my death, then its power would be diminished. It would be uncertain when I would die, and even whether I would die. This would give me a certain anxiety. But it would also give me some hope. If my death were escapable, then I wouldn't necessarily have to deal with my mortality. Or, better, I would deal with my mortality, but I could do so by trying to avoid it rather than simply come to terms with it. This is not the same kind of anxiety as knowing that I will certainly die, but not knowing when.

Conversely, if I were to know when I would die, this would offer a different kind of anxiety. There is a cruelty said to be associated with the death penalty that consists in knowing when one will die. There seems to be something right about this. Part of what is right about it, though, is that the certainty of one's death lies in the near future rather than the far future. It is not the same thing to know that one will die in several months rather than in forty years. To know one will die in forty years, and not less, gives a certain kind of comfort

– at least for a good part of those years. At least one doesn't have to worry about dying *during* the next forty years. That is, to be sure, a difficult situation to imagine. Does it mean I could drive my car off a cliff and not worry about it? Of course, the difficulty we have in imagining this situation tells us that the uncertainty of our death is a feature of our existence.

What is the particular anxiety associated with the combination of the inescapability and the uncertainty of death? The idea behind this combination is that we will certainly die, and that it can happen at any time. This means that death is always with us. It haunts us. It accompanies every moment of our lives. We are never far from death, because it will inevitably happen and we cannot control the moment when it will.

Of course, we are not always thinking about death. In fact, most of us avoid thinking about our death. But to avoid thinking about something does not mean it isn't there, helping to shape who we are and how we go about our lives. This is particularly true with unpleasant matters. We do not have to embrace psychoanalysis or believe in some concept of the unconscious to recognize that people often neglect to face things that are nevertheless influencing how they behave. Think, for instance, of how you try to gain the approval of certain types of people, for reasons you don't entirely understand, or of how you avoid certain kinds of situations – crowds or alone-ness, competitive or cooperative environments, work or leisure – without really knowing why you do so. Sometimes, something happens to let you know why: an association with a traumatic past event or the influence of someone you once knew. You don't need to endorse the idea that there is this place called the unconscious where these associations and influences come to rest. And you don't need to think that there is some special psychological procedure you need to go through to recall them. (And you certainly don't need to see them as stemming from some Oedipal complex.) We all know that things happen that we'd rather not think about, and that nevertheless those things are part of our past, stored somewhere in our memory. From there, it is not a far step to recognize that if those things are part of who we are, then they might have an effect on how we conduct ourselves.

So it is with death. We know we will die and we know that we don't know when we will die. We navigate our lives in the shadow of this dual recognition, without always bringing it before ourselves consciously and without always wanting to bring it before ourselves consciously. Our mortality is always at work within us, even when, or perhaps most especially when, we try to avoid it.

There are many ways to try to avoid this recognition. One could hew to one side of the recognition or the other. We shall return to this idea in the last part of this book, so for the moment a couple of quick examples will suffice. One could hew to the side of recognizing the uncertainty without recognizing the inevitability by always planning for the future, never living in the moment. If I always keep my eye on what is going to happen next, then I refuse to recognize that some day there will not be a next. Eventually those things that I have put off into the future will be frustrated, because there will come a day when there is no future, nor even a present. On the other side of things, I imagine (and maybe I'm wrong here) that more extreme types of mountain-climbers embrace the inevitability but balk at the uncertainty. This is because, at least the way I imagine it, by putting themselves in death's way they seek to master their own deaths: not by avoiding it, but precisely the opposite – by courting it. Death will happen to them, but on their own terms. Its uncertainty will be at least partially vanquished.

This is probably also what happens when we plan for our death, for instance, by making wills or taking our life insurance. Although we don't control our death in this way, we seek to control its effects on people we love.

Heidegger thinks that most people conduct their lives most of the time through a denial of death. He doesn't mean that people don't dwell on it all the time. In fact, some people do. But dwelling on death can also be a form of denial, since dwelling on it can be a way of trying to control it. (If I dwell on my death, keeping it always before me, then, as with my imagined extreme mountain-climbers, it can't sneak up on me and catch me unaware.) What he means is that we don't sufficiently come to terms with the fact of our death, with its finality, its goal-lessness, its inevitability and its uncertainty. Death helps structure our lives – it may be the most influential motivator in our lives – and yet we don't reflect on it, don't take it into account in considering the shape our lives take. He may be right about this. I suspect he is. When I taught the seminar on death I often woke up in the middle of the night in a cold sweat, thinking about the end of my existence. I don't generally do that. (My wife assures me that I sleep soundly and snore vigorously.) Thinking about death is something most of us would prefer to avoid. It makes us confront ourselves in a way we would rather not. And it raises a possibility that we would rather not consider: that our lives do not really have a meaning or a point.

This is the fourth aspect or theme of death. It is not, strictly speaking, a fact about death in the same way as the other three themes. It is more like a consequence that seems at times to flow from them. Death is final. It is a stoppage without goal or wholeness. It is inescapable and yet incalculable. It is not itself meaningless, but it can make us feel ourselves to be meaningless. We should ask ourselves why this is so. It isn't necessarily the case. As we shall see in the next part of the book, there is something about death that also lends significance or meaning to human life. But, confronted with the fact of death, we often feel as though our living has been in some way in vain. This is what needs investigation at the moment.

The sense of meaninglessness stems from the other three themes. We might articulate those themes in this way. First, death is the end of us. Nothing remains of us after we die. We are only the lives we lead now. Those lives have no point other than themselves. They lead to nothing else: no reward, no punishment. All roads lead only to our annihilation. Moreover, and this is the second theme, death itself lends no meaning to those lives. In death, the threads that have tied us to the world are not knotted together or woven into some greater fabric. They are simply cut, left to lie there with no pattern or connection. Thirdly, this death that cuts those threads could happen at any time. There is no justice in when it happens, although happen it will. We live always in the recognition, if not the reflective awareness, that our lives will some day come to a cessation without closure and without appeal. And that that day could be any day. Some days may be less likely than others, but any day might do.

Put this way, death casts a shadow over our lives. And while I don't think this is the only way we might put it – we will see other ways of putting it – I also don't think this way is mistaken. We may view death in other ways, but these ways will not so much substitute for this way of seeing things as stand alongside it. What we have isolated here, in casting the three themes as we just have, is not an illusory view of the role of death in our lives. It is instead an accurate view of one aspect of that role. For many people, if this view is accurate, it would also be exhaustive. There would be nothing else to say.

Why? Most of us would like our lives to have a meaning or significance. We would like them to have a point. It is not enough to say that a life was fun, or that it was enjoyable while it lasted. This is not to say that fun and enjoyment have no role to play in a life. A joyless life would not be something anyone would probably want to live. But it seems as though there should be more.

That *more* could be had in a number of ways. It could be had through an afterlife that would make this life a trial or a preparation or a preliminary. In that way, a human life would assume its significance in regard to what happens afterwards. This might seem to diminish the importance of what happens during one's temporal existence. In his writings, the philosopher Friedrich Nietzsche criticizes religion precisely on this point. Religion, for him, is the attempt to denigrate our world in the name of some superior transcendent one. However, afterlives don't only diminish temporal lives; they also lend them significance. They offer lives the possibility of being successes and failures, which in turn allows these lives to make sense to those who live them.

The *more* that we seek could also be had in other ways as well. Suppose it would be possible to create one's life to be a work of art. That would seem to give it a beauty that would be meaningful. One's life could be like a novel, having a recognizable beginning, middle and end, where the end would allow us to pull the novel's elements together and see the meaning of the whole. Or it could be like a painting or music, where each of the life's themes engaged the others, like colours or notes, so that the whole assumed a radiance or a balance that might not be seen if one focused solely on the individual elements. In contrast to lives dedicated to an afterlife, here life would assume its significance in itself rather than in relation to something else. Nevertheless, it would have a significance, one that would be recognizable to the person who lived it.

Death frustrates both of these projects of lending life meaningfulness, of giving it that *more* that we seek. In the case of the afterlife, of course, we have not argued that there is no afterlife. How could one argue that? We have taken death to be the end of life, and have asked what it would mean to do so. So the possibility of an afterlife has been laid aside. The more nearly aesthetic option seems also to be precluded. Death, we have seen, does not give life a wholeness. It does not realize a goal; it just happens. Moreover, the attempt to turn one's life into a work of art seems to run counter to death's operation. We have seen that death does not bring together the threads of one's life. It merely cuts them. The best one can hope for then, from most lives, would be the creation of an unfinished work of art. At the end of almost every life, there will be colours or notes left unpainted or unplayed, themes not fully articulated. The beauty of the whole will go missing.

Some might object that there are other ways for a life to assume meaning. It can, for instance, be dedicated to the good of others. Both of the ways we have considered here look upon a life on its own terms. They both judge a life in abstraction from its context. Perhaps we must think of the meaningfulness of a life differently. It is not in relation to itself that life has its importance, but rather in its contribution to the world, and specifically to others who inhabit that world. Perhaps the first two ways of seeking the significance of a life are too self-contained or self-involved.

I don't want to deny that human lives can take on meaning in this way. My goal here is not to say that death eliminates the very possibility of our lives' having meaning. Rather, it is to point to why death seems to lend an aura of meaninglessness to our lives. To that end, we can see two ways in which death can cast a shadow over the prospect of drawing meaning from one's contribution to the lives of others. The first has to do with the others themselves. If death makes life as contingent and pointless as we have cast it in our recent, darker summary of the three themes, then my desire to contribute to other lives is, ultimately, in vain. The lives of others are no more meaningful than my own. Contributing to them could not amount to anything more than an offer of minor comfort. It would be like sharing a meal with a fellow passenger on a sinking ship. The gesture may be a fine one, but it doesn't make the situation any less dire.

To see this clearly, we can reverse the situation. Suppose I view my life in light of death as we have described it. I take my life to be finished by an inevitability that stalks me at every moment and whose arrival will serve only to destroy everything I have built. What can others contribute that would ameliorate my condition? The problem is not that I lack something that can be provided by others. It is that I am going to die. And, since no one can take my death away from me, no one can contribute in a deep way to my living.

The other way death casts a shadow on the attempt to live life as a contribution to others has to do less with those others than with oneself. It is difficult to take one's meaning *solely* through the flourishing of others. We want to feel as though our lives had meaning in some sense on their own terms. This is what makes the first two ways we looked at — afterlives and artistic lives — attractive. Even if we take these ways of creating meaningfulness to be too self-centred (although we haven't argued that they are), they do capture something central about how we think about the shape of our lives. We need not be selfish or haughty to want to think of our lives as taking on a significance that is not reducible to our contribution to others' lives. To put the point another way, most of us do not want to think of the meaning of our lives vicariously: our lives are not merely the vehicle for the thriving of others. This does not mean that we must think of ourselves before others or above others. We can very well think of ourselves *alongside* others. We are one among those who seek meaning. The meaningfulness of our own lives does not matter more than that of others, but nor does it matter less.

If we define our lives solely by our contribution to others, then we miss this dimension of meaningfulness. There may be some for whom this dimension is not important, but I doubt there are many. And among those few, there are probably much fewer still who do not believe in an afterlife or in the artistic quality of what they're doing. But if this dimension is important, then we return to face the same problem of meaninglessness that death has brought before us. We are summoned before death without the resources to construct a life that would be meaningful on its own terms, and so have not advanced in our ability to give our mortal lives a point.

Baldly put, the dual problem facing those who would characterize the significance of a mortal life in terms of its contribution to others is that if the others are mortal there is no such thing as a real contribution and, even if there were, it would not solve the problem of how one's own life is to have significance, aside from its contribution to others.

We can see then why the subject of death is mostly faced through avoidance. It presents a threat to the core of our sense of who we are and how we think of ourselves. Faced with death, most of us, as Heidegger puts the point, live in the mode of fleeing it. In particular, we flee what he calls the *Angst*, the anguish, we experience in the face of death. Anguish is what happens to us when we are faced with what he calls "the possibility of our impossibility". It is the sense that accompanies my recognition that I am going to fall into a void, that my experience will end, and that I have little control over when and how and no control over whether this will happen. I have slightly expanded Heidegger's idea here. It is not only death itself, but the meaninglessness that seems to leach from it, that gives us anguish.

We would rather not face death and the anguish we feel from it. So we choose ways of living that keep the recognition of death at bay. Although we humans are the kinds of creatures that recognize our mortality, we usually comport ourselves as though we did not. We live as though death and its threat of meaninglessness were no concern of ours. Marcus Aurelius, the Roman emperor and Stoic philosopher, like other ancient philosophers, sought to keep the idea of death in front of him, in order that he could order his daily activities in a more appropriate way. We will return to Aurelius's approach to death later, but for now we should recognize that for many ancient philosophers the fact of death as a central element of human being needs to be grappled with if one is to live a worthy life. A worthy life, after all, cannot be lived by one who is in the grip of an illusion.

Of course, most of Aurelius's contemporaries, just like most of us, do not try to integrate our mortality into life. We seek precisely to disintegrate it. We have many ways of doing this. Mostly, we ignore death. We plan for the future as though it were not going to happen. We conduct ourselves like other animals whose awareness of death arises only when they face an imminent threat. We know in some sense that we are going to die. We know that our death will be the end of us, that death is not an accomplishment or a goal, and that it is at once inevitable and uncertain. And yet we scurry about under this knowledge as though it had nothing to do with us. Death, when it comes, is always a shock, a blow from the outside, rather than the central human possibility. We react to death – that is, the death of others – as though it were something that happened to them, rather than something about who they are. If we saw it as the latter, we would equally have to see ourselves as mortal. For most of us, at least most of the time, that is too much to bear.

When we don't ignore death we seek to diminish its impact. If any of the religious traditions we discussed above are true, then the impact of death is surely blunted, because we don't really die. Our bodies perish and disintegrate, but our essential selves remain intact. We do not lose our souls, and thus in some sense our experience, the *who-ness* of who we are. Whether or not these traditions are true, however, belief in them is enough to keep the anguish death provokes at arm's length. This is one of the powers of faith. It allows one to embrace the comfort offered by religion in the absence of either ultimate proof or disproof of its doctrines.

There are, of course, weaknesses to these defences against the threat of death. We might ignore death for much of our lives but its evidence is everywhere around us. It does not cease to haunt us even when we pull the covers over our heads. The fact that we have so many ways of pulling the covers over our heads is itself evidence of death's pervasiveness. And religion, too, because for most it is an object of faith, cannot assure those who believe that all will be well. Faith struggles with doubt, giving death an opening. Belief can push against death, but doubt allows death to push back.

It seems that, in the final analysis, there would only be two cures for the central role death, and the anguish it provokes, plays in our lives. Since to be human is to be aware of death, we could hope to revert to a less conscious, less aware status. Becoming something other than human, something with a lesser cognitive capacity, would allow us to live death as though it weren't there. It would remove us from death's power: not *over* our lives, but at least *within* them. Few of those who have thought about death have embraced this possibility. This is probably because it would be intolerable to most of us to be something other than a human being. Most of us think of this something *other* as something *less*. We would think of a conversion to a less conscious mode of existing as a step or two down the evolutionary scale. I have avoided this way of talking, for two reasons. First, technically there is no evolutionary scale. What is adaptive in one environment is maladaptive in another. So what looks like an evolutionary advance in one situation would appear very different if environmental conditions were to change. Secondly, and partly because of this, to speak of the other as the lesser seems to imply an unnecessary disrespect for non-human animals. Since I have recently become a vegetarian, it would be unseemly of me to exhibit such disrespect. Nevertheless, the prospect of becoming something different from a human being, with full human consciousness, is one that few of us would endorse as a salve for the recognition of our mortality.

The other cure would not be a cure for the recognition of death. It would be a cure for death itself. If we were immortal, if we did not die, then everything about death that haunts our lives would immediately disappear. We would not have to worry about the end of our experience, because our experience would never end. The problems of ripeness and wholeness at the end of life would not arise. Death would not be inescapable and uncertain, because it would not be. And therefore the problems of meaninglessness attendant on death would not become a concern for us. In contrast to the possibility of not being aware of death, there are many who have thought about immortality. Or at least, as we shall see, they have tried to think about immortality. Immortality would no doubt cure the problem of death. Would it give our lives meaning? Would we be better off without death? In thinking through the problem of death, the problems it presents, we can sharpen up our views by contrasting death with immortality. We can ask, or at least seek to ask, how an immortal life might differ from the mortal ones that are our lot. In doing so, we might see death and the role it plays in our life from another angle. Perhaps this other angle will yield other insights, insights we can use to confront the fact that, in the end, each of us really is going to die.

2. Death and immortality

In the short story "The Immortal", the Argentinian writer Jorge Luis Borges tells the story of Joseph Cartaphilus. To be more accurate, Cartaphilus tells his own story, with Borges the narrator doing little more than setting the scene. Cartaphilus describes living in ancient Thebes, and crossing paths with a man who sought a river in Egypt that "cleanses men of death". The man soon dies, but Cartaphilus himself decides to seek this river, on the far side of which is the glorious City of the Immortals. He leads a group of men to find the river, but they mutiny against him and he is forced to flee. He goes to sleep one night and awakens with his hands bound and with a terrible thirst. He sees a small, brackish body of water below him, and throws himself into it. His thirst is slaked, but he is so weak he cannot move. Days pass, but he does not know how many.

Meanwhile, he is surrounded by beings he calls *troglodytes*: wizened, stooped men without speech who "devoured serpents". They do nothing to help him, but instead merely watch as he struggles to survive. Eventually, he frees himself and sets his path towards the City of the Immortals. He wanders through the environs of the troglodytes, hoping that at their outskirts will lie the great city. Instead he finds a vast labyrinth with little more than ruins. As he wanders, he is followed by one of the troglodytes, whom he names Argos, after Ulysses's dog in the *Odyssey*. One day the troglodyte speaks, telling Cartaphilus about the character of the dog Argos. Cartaphilus asks the troglodyte what he knows of the *Odyssey*, and the troglodyte replies that he invented it. Cartaphilus's Argos is, in actuality, Homer.

The troglodytes are the immortals, and the City of the Immortals is nothing more than the ruins through which Cartaphilus has been wandering. Having drunk from the river at the base of the city, Cartaphilus too is now immortal. He records his exploits in later years, including his puzzlement and uncertainty about this record. The story ends with a postscript that casts some doubt on the record itself, as well as the narrator's defence of the record as an immortality of words.

What is striking, however, particularly for our purposes, is Cartaphilus' depiction of the troglodytes and the City of the Immortals. He writes that the labyrinth through which he wandered had replaced the earlier, more glorious city. The Immortals had razed the city and built the labyrinth as a kind of parody of religion, the irrationality of its passages contrasting with the rationality mortals ascribe to the gods. Moreover, the labyrinth was the last great project undertaken by the Immortals: for them "it marks a stage at which, judging that all undertakings are in vain, they determined to live in thought, pure speculation. They erected their structure, forgot it and went to dwell in the caves".

Why, for the Immortals, are all undertakings in vain? Given an infinite amount of time for existence, everything will happen of its own accord. There is nothing an immortal being cannot eventually do; and, in fact, nothing he or she will not eventually do. Cartaphilus writes, "Homer composed the *Odyssey*; if we postulate an infinite period of time, with infinite circumstances and changes, the impossible thing is not to compose the *Odyssey*, at least once." If one is going to live forever, there is, in the literal sense, time for everything.

This tells us why the Immortals chose to live in pure thought rather than in the physical world. For mortal beings, as we have seen, life is fraught. What happens is fragile. It might not have happened. Or it might have happened without our experiencing it. It could have happened somewhere else, or before or after our lives. The events of our lives, both good and bad, have an urgency that they do not have for the Immortals. An Immortal does not worry about missing anything. There is time for it to be experienced. In fact, there is time for it to be repeatedly, infinitely, experienced. For those of us who die, there is a singularity to the moments of our existence. For the Immortals, by contrast, there is only repetition: Cartaphilus explains that "among the Immortals, on the other hand, every act (and every thought) is the echo of others that preceded it in the past, with no visible beginning, or the faithful presage of others that in the future will repeat it to a vertiginous degree."

This is why the physical world does not interest them. If they have not seen it all, they will. There is nothing to strive for, no act that confers meaning. The world unfolds, good passing into bad, bad passing into good. Seen from the longest point of view, there is little to distinguish good from bad. So instead of striving to accomplish something in this world, the Immortals withdraw into a world of pure speculation. One might point out that, given enough time, pure speculation would also be repetitive. My interpretive suspicion here is that what is at issue in pure speculation is not the activity of speculating but instead the withdrawal from action. One speculates, not as a thinker, but as a spectator. One watches the spectacle take place before one, not entirely interested in the proceedings.

Why the labyrinth, though, with its implicit critique of religion? Why do the Immortals parody religion with a monument to irrationality? For most religions, there are distinctions to be made between good and bad. Mortality offers meaning to the events of our lives, and morality helps us navigate that meaning. If one lives a limited amount of time, then it matters how one lives and acts. That is the urging of religion: to make of this life something that matters in the right way. It is not contradicted by what we saw in Chapter 1: that religion tries to confer immortality. Even if you survive your death, you do not survive your earthly life, or, with the approach to Buddhism we discussed, your particular earthly life. Each life is a test for the next one. This does place meaning and significance on this life. In that sense, religion has it both ways: there is meaning to this life as a prelude to the next, but also the immortality of one's continued existence.

For the Immortals, there is no such meaning and significance because their immortality is precisely here, in this life. This life is not a test or a prelude. It is all there is. And, without limits, this life cannot take on the meaning that religion finds in it. As a result, the universe seems less rational than it does to a religion of mortal life. The meaning found in the latter does not exist for the former. Without meaning, immortal life becomes irrational. The gods who designed the universe, then, seemed less inclined to have created an orderly universe where everything has its place, but instead to have created a universe without point or meaning. In this universe, one wanders aimlessly forever, crossing and re-crossing paths that add up to no particular pattern. What better way to reflect this than by building a labyrinth that leads nowhere?

Borges's story suggests much, and I have offered only a quick interpretive gloss here. If we are to think through the idea of immortality, at least as best we can, we need to tug a little more systematically at some of the threads we have isolated here. It is, of course, difficult to think about immortality. It is necessarily speculative. Given the ideas we have seen in the first part of the book, it is not difficult to see why. If, as I have argued, death is the central fact of human life, then it becomes difficult to imagine human life without it. In some sense, an immortal life is no longer a human life. Borges captures that idea when he describes the Immortals as troglodytes.

Nevertheless, alongside the fact of mortality we have seen the difficulty of facing death. Human beings, aware of our impermanence, are also weighted by it. We desire not to die. But the desire not to die may not be exactly the same thing as the desire for immortality. To see the difference, we need to investigate immortality more rigorously.

Perhaps the best place to start is by returning to a characteristic that is central for the human relation to death. Humans are not the only creatures that die: all organisms do that, sooner or later. We are creatures who know that we will die, and who know it throughout our lives, even when we aren't in imminent danger. It may be that other creatures also know this, but we certainly do. If we take that characteristic and apply it to immortality, we can ask about immortality with and without consciousness of immortality. In other words, we can imagine humans as immortal in at least two ways. First, we can imagine, or at least try to imagine, immortal human beings who do not recognize their immortality. Then we can imagine immortality with awareness of that immortality.

For Joseph Cartaphilus, unawareness of death is itself a sort of immortality. It is distinct, though, from the type of immortality one is aware of. "To be immortal is commonplace; except for man, all creatures are immortal, for they are ignorant of death; what is divine, terrible, incomprehensible, is to know that one is immortal." Let us ask first about this immortality without awareness. Cartaphilus here is not talking about immortality without awareness of one's immortality. He is talking about mortality without awareness of one's mortality, and equating *that* with immortality. What is the equation? In this view, death only takes hold of us when we become aware of it. It is not, of course, that we need to be aware of our dying in order actually to die. Rather, it is that death would not become part of who we are if we were unaware of the fact of our dying. In one sense, without such awareness we would not be mortal creatures: we would not be creatures for whom our mortality would be an important fact about us. If, alternatively, it is a central fact about us, it is precisely because of that awareness.

While it may be stretching things a bit to say that animals without awareness of death are immortal, we might say that they are at least in some sense non-mortal. They die, but their dying is not a fact that shapes who or what they are.

Might we think of human immortality without awareness this way? Might there be a sense in which human beings, if immortal and yet unaware of their immortality, are best described as non-mortal? I don't think we can make that analogy so quickly. If it is a central fact about us that we are aware of our death, then it is hard to imagine what we would be like without that awareness. Something important to our humanity would go missing were we to lose the consciousness of our perishability. Does this mean as well that we cannot imagine human immortality without awareness? And that such a condition would no longer be human?

I suspect this is probably true, or close to true. We can think of it this way. Part of what gives death its significance is that, as we have seen, human beings project their lives out into the future. Plans are made, commitments undertaken, relationships cultivated, all with an eye to their future unfolding and development. Our consciousness of our mortality lends a certain precariousness to those plans, commitments and relationships. It's not that we don't participate in them, but we participate as beings haunted by death. Now let's imagine the situation with immortality. We would still be committed to projecting our futures, but those futures would not look the same. They would not be clouded by the fragility that death brings, or have the urgency associated with knowing that they are marked by the limitations of time. We would participate in our endeavours without having to take account of these parameters.

If this were all, then we would be non-mortal, in the sense we described in the last paragraph. Immortality would not figure in our lives. But it is hard to see how this could be all. To project into the future the way that we do requires that we have some sense of the shape of that future. We know, or at least think we know, what it is going to look like in a broad sense. This does not mean that we can predict the future. But there are certain things we can say about it. The eighteenth-century British philosopher David Hume argues that human beings assume the future will resemble the past in the sense that what seem to be causal relations will continue to hold. If material bodies seem to be held together by gravitational force, that will not suddenly come to an end in the near future.

Immortality is like causality in this way. Just as we assume that what appear to be the causal relations of our world will continue to hold, if we were immortal we would live as though the future would keep unfolding without end. We would project out into the future as an immortal being would. We would form our plans, commitments and relationships in light of the fact that the future will just *keep going*. And what is that but the awareness of immortality?

The point I'm insisting on here is that the awareness of death is not some free-standing awareness for human beings. We saw this in Chapter 1. Its spectre emerges from within the way we live, haunting the commitments we make. Were humans incapable of projecting out into the future, death would have a very different role to play from the one it does. So it would be with immortality. The ability to project into the future in the way humans do requires some sense of what that future looks like, at least in very broad outline. It would seem to be inevitable, then, that creatures who orient themselves towards the future as humans do would be aware of whether that future was or was not going to end. We are either aware of our mortality or aware of our immortality.

One might press this issue in at least two directions. First, one might ask whether other creatures aside from humans project out into the future in the way we do, and thus are likely to be aware of their deaths – or, in the imaginative example we are considering, aware of their immortality. I do not want to deny that this is possible. It seems to me that evolution might well yield creatures that have a conscious engagement in their futures and therefore some awareness of death. Chimpanzees might fall into this category, or perhaps dolphins. It is not my goal to show that human beings are entirely different from all other animals when it comes to death. I'm concerned with our relation to death, with the human relation to it. If it turns out that there are other animals with this kind of awareness, that would indicate a deeper sharing we would have with these animals.

The other way to press the issue is to ask what would happen if humans did not project out into the future in the way that we do. This, I believe, would be a less interesting route to follow. In order to do so, we would have to imagine human beings without a relation either to death or immortality and without a relation to the future of their commitments. Beings like this no longer have much in common with us. We might ask about what their lives would look like under conditions of immortality, but it would not help us think about our own relation to death, about a *human* relation to death. It's not even clear, given how different such creatures would be, that we could go very far in imagining their lives in the first place.

We find ourselves, then, with only one real imaginative option: to consider human beings who are both immortal and aware of their immortality. We need to ask what it would be like to be us, just as we are, with one central change: that we are not going to die. Of course, our not dying would change many things about us. But what we want to ask is how things would change for us and about us on the basis of our immortality alone. We want to ask what effect immortality would have on us. In order to do that, we take ourselves as we are, introduce this single variation and then ask how it changes us. Immortality, then, is like a value we might introduce for a variable in an equation, where we are the equation. We substitute that value for x, and see what happens to the equation.

In doing so, we should probably distinguish between immortality and what is often referred to as *eternity*. Sometimes the two terms are used in the same way, but not always. When they're used differently, immortality is considered to be living throughout or across time while eternity is taken to be stepping outside of time. If one is immortal, then one is always alive. To exist in eternity is to be immune to time, if only for a little while. Our concern here is with immortality rather than eternity in this sense. Eternity can happen to someone who is either mortal or immortal, as in having moments that are eternal, that seem to stand outside of time. And if we think of eternity in terms of an afterlife, then we are back in the religious traditions that we considered in Chapter 1.

In asking about immortality, however, there is another imaginative hurdle we must clear. It is not enough to imagine us as immortal; we must ask *how* we are to be immortal. Specifically, we must ask about the aging process. Human life, if it is not cut short, involves a physical development and a decline. Physical development does not necessarily mirror emotional or intellectual development. Many, although by no means all, of us become more emotionally stable as our bodies lose their vigour. And intellectual development is independent of both physical and emotional development. For musical and mathematical creativity, it is said that the peak occurs early, while for philosophy it is often said to be later. Moreover, all of these past few statements are generalizations. In my case, for instance, physical development went into a trough in late adolescence and didn't return until my mid-forties. This is because I sustained a back injury when I was sixteen, and it took twenty-five years or so before I was able to return to the kind of athletic condition I had before the injury. This, I should hasten to add, was not because of the depth of the injury. I had a herniated disc, which is now cured with an outpatient procedure. The problem was a lack of knowledge about how to treat and recover from the injury, so I wound up being more sedentary than I should have been for many years.

In any case, if we are to consider immortality, we need to fix the parameters of human development in order to get a clear picture of what we are to imagine. Borges's character Joseph Cartaphilus does not offer any clues in this regard. He seems to be old enough to engage in reflective activity, but there are no references to his physical condition. By contrast, in *Gulliver's Travels*, Jonathan Swift imagines a race of immortals called the struldbrugs. The struldbrugs do not die, but they do age. They live a fairly normal human life until about age thirty, at which point they start a physical decline. That decline continues, eventually leading to blindness and other ills of old age. However, they remain alive. Moreover, their immortality stands as a threat to those around them, who worry that, given enough time and given the avarice of old age, the struldbrugs will gain a proprietary monopoly on all the social resources. Therefore, at the age of eighty their property is automatically passed on to their heirs and they are considered legally dead.

In depicting immortality this way, Swift certainly makes it appear unappealing. Of course, we need not picture immortality as a continuous physical decline. How we ought to picture it depends on what we're interested in asking. Let's recall the driving question for this part of the book. It is motivated by where we left off in the previous chapter. Dying, it seems, is an evil for us. Its characteristics of finality, goallessness and inevitability combined with uncertainty lead to the threat of feeling our lives to be without significance. In this light, we ask whether it would be better not to die.

Given this motivation, it is probably best not to imagine ourselves in the position of the struldbrugs. In wanting to continue to live, we don't seek simply biological existence. It is not just a matter of having our blood circulating and our limbs moving. And it is not simply a matter of being a spectator to the world. (Although, as we saw in Chapter 1, being a spectator at times does have its merits. That is what the philosopher Nagel pointed to, and which I tried to capture with the example of waking up from a nap and enjoying the colours of the leaves against the sky.) It is also a matter, as we have seen, of being able to continue participating in our plans, our commitments and our relationships. What dying threatens, in large part, are these elements of our lives: the ongoing engagement in and projection into the future of the threads that constitute our individual existences. As we saw in Chapter 1, death cuts off our future, and in doing so leaves those threads lying scattered about.

Moreover, this can happen at any time. And finally, we know this, even when we hide it from ourselves, at every moment.

If we are to imagine immortality as a cure for death, then, it must be an immortality that allows us to remain vibrant: one that at least keeps us physically vigorous and leaves room for emotional and intellectual development. It cannot be either an eternal childhood in which we do not understand the full possibilities a human life can offer, nor a decrepitude in which we cannot carry out the involvements in which a vital human life consists.

Here we can set some parameters, although your intuitions on this may differ from mine. I imagine a person in his or her early to mid-thirties, but perhaps even a little older, say late thirties. For some, this might be too old: mid-twenties may capture the point of physical and intellectual peak. My own view of this, I'll readily admit, might be skewed by my own athletic latency during my twenties, and also by the fact that I'm now in my fifties. However, we need not quibble here. We can imagine immortality keeping us at some period between the mid-twenties and late-thirties, give or take. The important thing is that immortality yields what death deprives us of: the ability to cultivate our plans, commitments and relationships. This seems to be, although Borges does not say so explicitly, where Joseph Cartaphilus finds himself.

Would such an immortality be worth having? There are at least some initially attractive features of it. First, and most significantly, it allows us to think about continuing the threads of our lives without their being cut off. One could devote oneself to one's relationships without concern for the death of one or another of those involved in those relationships. Time could be spent away from a loved one without wondering about the trade-offs that time would involve. A route back would always, temporally at least, be available. This does not mean that the relationship itself would not grow, or would not need to be reconfigured. It could be that experiences had while apart need to be integrated into a relationship. At the extreme, it could be that those experiences threaten a relationship. An affair can threaten a love relationship; experiences gained by travel can make an erstwhile friend seem too provincial. However, if the desire exists on both sides, it would always be possible to find a way back to a relationship, and perhaps even one enhanced by time apart.

In ancient China, those who were groomed to be the country's bureaucrats were all schooled together. They formed deep and abiding friendships, friendships of the kind that can happen when people feel they have encountered their intellectual and social peers. However, after their education, these bureaucrats were scattered to the various corners of China in order to perform their roles as functionaries. For many of them, the most significant relationships of their lives would be those formed during their school years. Over the course of their careers they would write one another letters. These communications often involved a plan for a rock garden. These Chinese functionaries would, throughout their working lives, design and modify plans for a rock garden in which they would all come together to live after their retirement. They would design the garden and the rooms, they would pick a location in which it was to happen and they would commission the building of the garden. This was a way of keeping them involved in a common project and of promising them a future together during the (often lonely) years of service in the far corners of the Chinese empire.

There are contemporary equivalents to this practice, although they are rarely implemented. There was once talk among some of my old friends of getting a common apartment, a large loft space, in New York, one that we could all retire to, or at least have access to when we get older. That talk has faded with the years, though. As children take up time and energy and careers grow, the city we grew up in becomes, for those of us that left it for one reason or another, a dream more of the past than of the future.

Why such dreams, though? There are things that have occurred in our lives, periods through which we have lived, that possess a special meaning to us. A good part of the reason for this is that we went through those periods with people we cared about. We formed relationships that had significance for us. In many cases they still do, even if the relationship no longer exists. What the ancient Chinese bureaucrats understood was both the singularity of those relationships and their vulnerability to distance. The communal designing of the rock gardens was a way to maintain the relationships in a common endeavour and at the same time to give them hope for an eventual return to something like the time in which those relationships were born.

Immortality would render such arrangements superfluous, because it would keep the door always open to picking up the relationships. There would be no need to plan for old age, because there would be no old age. There would be no need even to fix a time in which to meet again, because there would always be time. It might be that the thickness of experience would drive people's interests in divergent directions, so that finding a common space would no longer be an enjoyable project. But that is not a fault to be laid at the doorstep of immortality. Growing apart happens to us mortals all the time. It would be no more likely to occur if we were immortal. We would have access to what the ancient Chinese functionaries sought, with the addition that we could do it anywhere or at any time, circumstances permitting. Moreover, on the assumption we're working with – that immorality does not age us physically – we would have the energy to cultivate those relationships once we resumed them.

We have been discussing here a single aspect of immortality: that it protects the threads of our lives from being cut. This goes a long way towards addressing the concerns we raised about death in Chapter 1. Immortality would stymie concerns associated with the second and third themes that we discussed there. It would allow for every project to be accomplished, circumstances permitting. At least it would not undercut those projects for lack of time. To be sure, many among us will never be great basketball players or poets, even given all the time in the world. But the second theme did not concern just any endeavours at all; it concerned the projects in which each of us is actually engaged. Those projects could be seen through to their eventual success or failure.

The third theme concerned the uncertainty and yet inevitability of death, and the haunting of our lives that that involves. Immortality would end that haunting, because the only inevitability we would face with death would be that it wasn't going to happen. As that haunting concerned the threads of our lives being cut prematurely, the aspect of immortality we're discussing now would also allay that worry.

There are other attractive aspects of immortality as well, although the central ones are bound to the aspect we've just seen. Another one worth discussing regards choice. We learn as we grow older that one cannot be everything one wants to be. One must make choices. I would have liked to be a novelist, and have even written a couple of manuscripts. However, I could not become a novelist and a philosopher, and circumstances led me towards the latter. (I know that there are those who accomplish both, but they have skills I don't possess.) All of us, at some point or another, let go of futures we have envisaged for ourselves: we cannot follow two distinct career paths at the same time; we must put food on the table; for many of us, one thing just leads to another. We wake up one morning recalling there was a time we considered being a musician or opening a cafe or working our way across the country or the world taking on odd jobs. And, for one reason or another, it's too late for that now.

If we were immortal, we would not face those choices. Our lives would not be constrained by the choices we do make, because we would be able to make others. I could be a philosopher and then be a novelist. I could ride a bike from New York to Arizona, as I once hoped I would. Infirmity and mortality would not impose on me the necessity of selection. In this sense, it would eliminate one of the great sadnesses of life: regret. It would not eliminate all regret, of course. I could still, for instance, do things to others that I would come to regret. However, there is a certain and devastating kind of regret that immortality would eliminate. A teacher of mine once said that the saddest thing in life, aside from parents having to bury their children, is to lie on one's deathbed and have regrets. You know the kind of regrets he was referring to. Not regrets about what or who one could have become. Often we can't control who or what we can become. The kind of regrets he meant were those associated with who or what one *tried* to become or, better, *allowed oneself* to try to become. To fail to become something one works or trains or educates oneself for is a disappointment. But it pales in comparison to the regret of wondering whether one could have been *that*, if one had only taken one's chances.

If we were immortal, we would not be subject to those regrets. (As a side benefit, we would also not have to worry about what my teacher called the saddest thing in life either, assuming immortality to be the general human condition.) There would always be time to try something. Or, better, as we saw with the issue of accomplishing one's projects, we would always be able to try it, given the circumstances. We would not, for instance, be able to be a classical musician if classical music disappeared from human culture. And there might be regret associated with that. One can imagine an immortal being who was alive three hundred years ago regretting three hundred years from now not having taken up classical music. Barring that, however, regret would not play the same role in an immortal life as it does in our actual mortal ones.

Immortality, then, would at the very least allow us to continue the threads of our lives, the engagements that characterize human being, and would blunt the force of a certain kind of regret. It would appear, then, that immortality would enhance our lives in crucial ways. An immortal life, by overcoming the difficulties associated with death, would make our lives more meaningful. Or so it seems.

What we have not really grasped yet is the temporal aspect of immortality. We have not come to terms with how long immortality really lasts. It is, after all, an infinite amount of time. We have investigated the way immortality circumvents the problems of closure that death brings. Death cuts us off from our possibilities, both the ongoing engagements of our lives and other projects we might not yet have embarked on. But eliminating closure is only one aspect of immortality. Another aspect, one that may challenge us as human beings, is that our lives keep going on and on.

Let us begin to imagine this, starting with the problem of regret. One of the things I would have liked to spend more time on is learning music, specifically jazz saxophone. When I was in my early forties, I took up jazz sax for several years. I was never particularly good at it, but I did get to play a couple of times with a local band. I wasn't bad at improvisation. My problem was that I kept playing my solos on the beat. In jazz, you have to be a little behind the beat; that's what gives it the quality of swing. I didn't develop the ability to stay behind the beat. Some of it could be my personality. I'm compulsive enough that the idea of letting myself get behind in anything provokes anxiety. Whether I could have eventually gone beyond that is something I never found out. The jazz group that let me play broke up, and I didn't have another opportunity on the horizon to play with others. Eventually, I sold my saxophone and used the money for a dog-sledding trip in the Arctic. (For the record, the sax I was working with at the end of my short career was a Selmer Mark VI: John Coltrane's model. I made a deal on it.)

I don't have great regrets about no longer playing, and don't think I'll wonder on my deathbed what I could have done if I had stuck with it. Moreover, I'm sure you can think of activities or hobbies like this one. They are more than passing fancies and less than important commitments. Now let's suppose I were immortal.

At some point I would probably return to the sax. Maybe I would learn to play behind the beat. It's unlikely I would have become very good at it, but suppose I had. Suppose I had been able to play for a while professionally. At some point, it would have been enough: I don't know when, but sooner or later. For me, probably ten or twenty years would do it. But you can make it as long as you like. Surely within a thousand years or so I would become pretty tired of playing. After all, this is not one of my important life goals.

But perhaps one can imagine it becoming an important life goal. It has happened before. I was not born doing philosophy. It's something that became a central part of my life over years of doing it. Couldn't it be the same with jazz saxophone? Couldn't I find myself far more immersed in it than I would have thought likely?

There is no reason to think that I couldn't. I might have decided to throw myself into jazz, staying up late at night to go to clubs, listening over and over again to old jazz records, practising with possibilities the horn has to offer. But for how long? Even if I became dedicated to the music, could I do it for a thousand years? Five thousand? At some point, it begins to strain credulity to believe that one could stay immersed in a practice for an infinite amount of time.

Does it, though? Great musicians practice for hours a day, day after day. They never seem to get tired of it. However, musicians, like the rest of us, are mortal. They throw themselves into what they are doing because they want to be as accomplished as possible in the limited amount of time they have to play. And that time is very limited: seventy to eighty years at the outside. Multiply that amount of time by ten. Then by a hundred. Then by a thousand. That is an awfully long time to be playing an instrument. And it would only be the beginning. There would always be more time to practice.

I have no proof here that immortality would bring boredom to playing music. How could there be proof one way or another? None of us is immortal, so we can't really know for sure. And we do know that there are projects and relationships that people carry on throughout their lives. So it seems as though that could just continue on into whatever future one had, even if it were an infinite one. Appearances here, however, are misleading. Even the deepest of passions is likely to fade with the passage of enough time. What was not eroded by decades will probably be eroded by centuries or millennia.

There is another problem immortality brings to commitment as well, one that is elucidated by Borges's story. When there is time for everything it is hard to make anything matter. One's engagements become less pressing. Why pick up the saxophone and play my scales today when there is an infinity of tomorrows in which to practise? Cartaphilus learns that the Immortals eventually razed their city to the ground. Why? They came not to matter. Everything will happen of its own accord; as a result, the Immortals became spectators to their own lives. They lost involvement in them and resorted to pure speculation. We shall return to the idea of pure speculation shortly. For now, the idea we want to focus on is the way immortality saps involvement in one's own commitments.

The philosopher Martha Nussbaum has reflected on this aspect of immortality: on what it does to a life. She argues that the clearest example we have in literature of human immortality is that of the Greek gods. Looking at their lives, she concludes that many of the virtues we associate with human life would go missing if we were immortal. Courage, for instance, would be absent, since it would be impossible to risk one's life for anything. Moderation would be less pressing, since our bodies would not be threatened by our activity. Even justice would be imperilled. The needs of others would not urge themselves on us in the same way, since their existence would not be threatened by our neglect. Indeed, among Borges's Immortals there is no strong imperative to help others. Homer tells Cartaphilus of a man who fell into a quarry and was left there for seventy years before anyone threw him a rope. His life was not in danger, but he spent those years "burning with thirst".

It is not only the virtues that would suffer. Personal relationships would change as well. They would become less serious, since less would be at stake. The bonds between parents and children would probably slacken if children were no longer dependent on their parents for survival. One might argue that they would need their parents for education and nurturance. This might be true, but even some elements of these could be acquired on one's own or through one's peers, given enough time. The same would be true of friendships. The activities I perform with a friend, the confidences I share, the vulnerability I display, the competition we provide for each other: all these things could still happen, but their significance would be diminished by the limitations my immortality places on my ability to sacrifice for him. Moreover, given an infinite amount of time, there would always be the possibility of the same kind of friendship with someone else: if not sooner, then later. There would always be time.

Nussbaum concludes that:

> the intensity and dedication with which very many human activities are pursued cannot be explained without reference to the awareness that our opportunities are finite, that we cannot choose these activities indefinitely many times. In raising a child, in cherishing a lover, in performing a demanding task of work or thought or artistic creation, we are aware, at some level, of the thought that each of these efforts is structured and constrained by finite time.   (1994: 229)

Immortality, then, threatens our engagements both externally and internally. Externally, it threatens them by dragging them on forever, beyond the human capacity to remain involved. Internally, it threatens them through a sort of psychological debilitation. The urgency we associate with our engagements, and urgency that stems from the fact that sooner or later we will have lost the time to complete or at least to participate in them, goes missing in immortality.

63

As a brief aside, let's return to the example of Chapter 1 of the parents whose child dies. I said at that point that the eventual death of the parents would structure how the parents lived their lives in light of the child's death. We can now see why this is. Imagine the parents as immortal and the child as not. That would be almost unimaginably worse than the parents' being mortal. It would combine the lack of serious engagement in one's ongoing projects that Nussbaum speaks of with eternal sadness at the child's death. Rather than being structured by a traumatic event that one must bear through the precariousness of one's own existence, their lives would be structured by a traumatic event that looms even larger, since there is nothing else very urgent to be attended to.

Returning to the current line of thought where everyone is immortal, one might object that there are always other things to do. Jazz saxophone is one among a myriad of activities I might throw myself into. There are always other things to try, other places to visit, other people to meet and learn about and get involved with. There are, it seems to me, two responses to this challenge. The first one is the easy philosophical response. The second one says a little more about us as individuals. The first response is this: there aren't always other things, places and people. There are many of them, to be sure. But the planet is a limited place with a limited number of practices. Sooner or later, one sees what there is to see, does what there is to do and meets whomever is around. It may take tens of thousands of years, or even a couple of hundred thousand. But sooner or later it's going to happen. (Actually, it might not happen with meeting new people, assuming they keep being born. This is a limit of speculating about immortality. For if people keep being born, where would they all live? For our purposes, however, this question is not pressing. We can reasonably assume that just meeting whoever happens to be born would not be a very fulfilling way to spend immortality.)

The other response depends on us as individuals. There are practices I'm interested in, and others I'm not. Philosophy, child-rearing,

running, basketball and, to a lesser extent, jazz fall on one side; golf, chemistry, fishing and ballet fall on the other. And they're not all. There are many activities I would be bored to have to participate in. If I did them because I could no longer stand the activities I had been passionate about, that would be a boring and meaningless existence. It would be like reading a book one isn't interested in just to pass the time because there's nothing else to read.

The idea here is that even if there were other activities available to us after our passions had dimmed, these activities do not consti-tute a valuable life, one that would bring us a sense of significance. Each of us is a particular historical trajectory with particular biolog-ical roots. This trajectory and these roots open up certain areas for us as being of interest, and close other areas down. None of us are interested in everything, nor could we be. Therefore, the external and internal threats to our engagements that immortality brings cannot be met simply by moving on to other practices. When what moves us most deeply is no longer a source of motivation, it is no comfort to be offered things that move us less deeply.

But what about just being alive, having experience? In Chapter 1 we followed Nagel's thought that experience itself is positive. Being alive, even in the absence of all projects and commitments, is itself positive. I tried to illustrate that thought with the example of waking up from a nap to find the green of tree leaves against the blue of the sky. Couldn't just being alive be enough? Even if all our projects lost their passion, would it not suffice to experience the passing moments?

I do not believe it would, and here we can bring evidence to bear. When I wake up from my nap, I will sometimes linger over the colours at the window: for ten, fifteen, even twenty minutes if I'm feeling a luxury of time – but not much longer than that. If I were forced to stay like that for a few hours it would become really unpleasant. I could not imagine years of it. Meditating is much the same. One can meditate for a period, but not for years at a time. For most of us, meditation serves, in good part, to allow us a measure of peace when we resume our activities. Meditation aids us in our lives; it is not a substitute for life. Bare experience, life without the emotional and intellectual involvement of our ongoing engagements, cannot be endured for very long. The mind, the body, have to move on. And if all they have to move on to are tasks without devotion, life becomes more of a burden than a passion.

It seems, then, that while Nagel may be right that experience is not neutral but rather positive, this positivity does not extend to immortality. Like our projects, pure experience cannot keep life worth living over an infinite period of time.

We can see now why the Immortals in Borges's story retreated into pure thought. Nothing in the world could move them, so they lived in caves and engaged in pure speculation. Pure speculation, it might seem, would offer some sort of ongoing activity that seems to have no end. After all, some topics at least offer the prospect of accommodating infinite thought. Mathematics, for instance, seems limitless in the possibilities it offers for proofs and demonstrations. So, too, imagination seems without boundaries. One could not practise music for an eternity, but couldn't one imagine musical variations without cease? Is it possible that an immortal life could exorcise boredom through an immersion in thought?

If anyone would endorse such a view, it is likely that it would be a philosopher. After all, thought is what philosophers do for a living. And, as I often discover when other people find out I'm a philosopher, there is a certain view of philosophers as people with their heads in the clouds, divorced from this world, nourished solely on our ideas. However, it is a philosopher, the recent British philosopher Bernard Williams, who disabuses us of such a view of philosophy and of the role of thought in sustaining an immortal life. Williams argues that, for philosophers as for other people, thought is not disengaged from the world. It is about the world. Its problems find their source in it, and it seeks to find a way to resolve puzzles and difficulties that arise for us while navigating through that world.

Think of the questions philosophers ask. What is justice? How should one live? What can I know? Are we free or determined? What is there? These questions may lead to other, more obscure questions. But they are founded on issues that arise for us in our lives. Physicists, chemists and biologists also find their questions in the world. They become curious about some aspect of the world, and so they investigate it. Perhaps the field of knowledge most abstracted from the world is mathematics. And even there, there are applications to this world, even though not all of mathematics requires it. (Could a pure mathematician be a good candidate for immortality?)

There is another way to put this point. Thought is in interaction with the other aspects of a person's life. In order for thought to be satisfying, it must intersect with those aspects in some way or another. This does not mean, for instance, that all philosophy must be applied philosophy. Rather, what it means is that my life and my thought cannot be entirely disengaged from one another. If I become curious about the structure of the world's existence, its ultimate matter, this curiosity is *my own*. It stems from and intersects with what we recently called my historical trajectory and my biological roots.

Williams writes, in an article on immortality entitled "The Makropoulos Case: Reflections on the Tedium of Immortality" (1976), that, for a person disposed to reflection, pure speculation:

> it seems quite unreasonable to suppose that those activities [what Williams calls "intense intellectual enquiry"] would have the fulfilling or liberating character that they do have for him, if they were in fact all he could do or conceive of doing. If they are genuinely fulfilling ... then the ground and shape of the satisfactions that the intellectual enquiry offers him, will relate to *him*, and not just to the enquiry. (*Ibid.*: 96)

It is one's life that leads one to certain questions. Those questions, although they may – and in philosophy, often do – take one far afield of one's original motivations, are nevertheless bound to those motivations, and must be sustained by them. Intellectual enquiry emerges from a person's life, and cannot be divorced from it. Therefore, to engage in intellectual enquiry solely for its own sake, and apart from any interests one might have, is not a life *I* could lead, because there would be no *I* there to lead it. Or, looked at from the perspective of an *I*, the pure speculation of the Immortals would not offer the ground of a satisfying life. Borges himself seems to suggest this in his depiction of the Immortals as troglodytes, whose world he does not make attractive. And Williams himself concludes, "The *Platonic introjection*, seeing the satisfactions of studying what is timeless and impersonal as being themselves timeless and impersonal, may be a deep illusion, but it is certainly an illusion" (*ibid.*).

Immortality, then, does not seem to offer the prospect of a meaningful or fulfilling life. Or, better, it does not seem to offer the prospect of a meaningful *human* life. We might imagine creatures who could engage in the same projects for an infinite period of time, or could take up projects without regard to their own personal histories and orientations, or could focus endlessly on their unfolding experience, or could immerse themselves in pure thought and speculation. But those creatures would not be us. They would not have lives of the sort we do, where our ongoing projects are rooted in who we are and the paths we have traversed to become who we are.

For humans, an immortal life would be shapeless. It would be without borders or contours. Its colour would fade, and we could anticipate the fading from the outset. An immortal life would be impossible to make *my* life, or *your* life. Because it would drag on endlessly, it would, sooner or later, just be a string of events lacking all form. It would become impossible to distinguish background from foreground. And, because we are aware of our immortality, all of this would probably happen sooner rather than later. Moreover, since our time would be endless, even if it did happen later, from the perspective of infinity it would have happened at the beginning, near the moment of our birth. As time stretches out endlessly, the events in it seem to get telescoped together towards the start, much as we make room for more shirts or coats in a closet by pushing everything to one side.

In "The Immortal", Homer describes the condition of mortality to Cartaphilus this way:

> Death (or its allusion) makes men precious and pathetic. They are moving because of their phantom condition; every act they execute may be their last; there is not a face that is not on the verge of dissolving like a face in a dream. Everything among the mortals has the value of the irretrievable and the perilous.

He says this from the perspective of one who knows better. The Immortals have seen it all, and they recognize that nothing is irretrievable, that everything will probably either happen again or happen in a similar way, and that from the larger perspective nothing is perilous either. We might turn this thought around though, and see it from the perspective of our mortality. It is precisely our mortality that gives the significance to our actions, that makes them important, that makes them matter.

Recall here the example of the Chinese rock garden. Was there not something that touches a chord among us in the project of a collective design done by people at a great distance from one another and that can only be realized in old age? If there is, it relies on the fragility of human life. We saw that with immortality, there would be no need for rock gardens like this. They would have no point. But if they had no point, would this really be a gain for our lives? Is human life enhanced when a collective project of this kind loses its meaning? Is it enhanced when the bonds between parents

69

and children, between friends, between people and what they do, is no longer serious and urgent, "precious and pathetic"? Is it not precisely because our faces are always on the verge of dissolving that what we do appears to us being worthy of our doing it?

It is death, then, that seems to give our life shape. The fact that we die is what makes what we do and who we do it with matter. This thought, of course, is in contrast to what we considered in Chapter 1, where death seemed not to improve but to diminish the meaning of our lives. There, death appeared as that which brings an arbitrary finality to our lives. It cuts the threads of our existence without allowing them to be bound together in a meaningful way. Death is what haunts us at every moment, threatening our engagements and our relationships with others. Here, by contrast, it is not death but immortality that menaces the meaningfulness of our lives. Externally and internally, immortality saps our passion, lowers the bar for our commitments, and leaves us, in the final analysis, bored with our own lives.

Both perspectives are right. Our lives are threatened by death, but not in such a way that they would be better if we were immortal. It is this idea we must understand in order to ask how to live with death, a question that Chapter 3 seeks to address. In order to understand it, we must be precise in our recognition of the ways in which death and immortality cast their shadows over our lives. For they do not do so in the same way.

Both death and immortality threaten the meaningfulness of our lives in part by the way they infuse them. But they infuse them differently. Death threatens our lives through incompletion. Our projects, commitments and relationships will just disappear, without being brought to accomplishment. But this is a problem for us only if those projects, commitments and relationships matter. If they did not matter, then their disappearance would not matter either. They would have no more significance than passing whims, which fade without regret. We might put the point this way. It is because our engagements matter to us that death takes on its menace. In that sense, and in light of the discussion of immortality we have had so far, death plays a dual role in the meaningfulness of our lives. On the one hand, it is death that lends our lives urgency and beauty. Without death, little seems to matter. With death, much does. On the other hand, death threatens the very meaningfulness it delivers. The fragility of our lives cuts in two directions. It both makes and unmakes the importance of those lives. It makes them in the sense that it lends an exigency to what we do: an irretrievability, a singularity and a uniqueness to the moments of our lives. It unmakes them in the sense of threatening that exigency and that singularity at every moment with annihilation.

Immortality works differently. It does not both make and unmake the meaningfulness of our lives. It simply unmakes them. Where death threatens that which it makes matter, immortality threatens the fact of mattering itself. It is not our projects and engagements, those that are important to us, that are at risk with immortality. It is, rather, the importance of those projects and engagements themselves. Commitments that drag on endlessly, events that hound us with their staggering repetition, alternatives that appear to us as pointless ways to pass the time: these do not so much destroy our lives through annihilation as cripple them through despair. With immortality, the threads of our lives are not exposed to being cut arbitrarily. Instead, those threads seem to have no particular colour and form: no particular pattern.

When we saw earlier how death was neither a goal nor an accomplishment we contrasted death with the ending of a novel. A novel's ending, at least most novels' endings, bring some sort of closure to the previous pages. It allows the reader to see the earlier parts of the novel in a certain light, giving those parts a particular gloss or orientation. At the very least, the ending of a novel plays a role in its structure and meaning. The ending of a novel is like a ripple on a pond whose effects move across the surface, giving the whole a certain appearance. Death is not like this. It does not bring life any closure or wholeness. It does not add meaning. It simply stops a human life from continuing.

Immortality can be contrasted with the novel's ending in a different way. With immortality, the novel never ends. It simply keeps going. There is no closure *to* the novel because there is no closing *of* the novel. But, like death, this lack of closure also results in a withdrawal of meaning. If a mortal life might be compared to an unfinished novel, one that the author has abandoned at some point along the way, immortality is to be compared to a novel that one must keep reading. Imagine this. Imagine a novel that you literally could not put down, but not because it is so interesting. It might be interesting for the first few thousand pages or so. But the reason you can't put it down is that you're forced to keep reading it. You can never finish it, because it does not end. The question is, what does that do to the significance of the novel? How meaningful can such a novel be? And, more to the point, what meaningfulness could it possibly have?

As it keeps unfolding, as the characters keep doing what they do and different situations keep appearing without cease, the novel itself begins to seem, in a word we have already invoked, *shapeless*. There is little that stands out from the rest, since there is nothing to make it stand out. Of course, the author (if we can even imagine the author of an infinitely long novel) may highlight certain themes, place certain recurrent images or situations before us, or repeat certain motifs. But as the novel keeps going, one wonders what the point of that highlighting or repetition might be. There is no whole into which it all fits, because there cannot be a whole.

As with the infinite novel, so with the immortal life. Somewhere along the way – a somewhere that we have noted will always appear to be at the beginning relative to the unending stretch of the life – the point of it all gets lost. If death refuses to bring the threads of a life together into a pattern because wherever they are cut is an arbitrary point, immortality refuses to allow them to be put into a pattern because it simply refuses to put them down.

This returns us to a disagreement between the philosophers Nagel and Williams. Nagel argues that experience itself is a good. Recall his idea that "what remains [if we leave aside the specific elements that make a life better or worse] ... is not merely *neutral*: it is emphatically positive". To be alive is a good thing. In any event, it beats the alternative. On this view, more life is better than less, not because of its quantity, but simply because it is life. Death, he argues, is an evil. It is an inevitable evil, but an evil nonetheless, because it deprives us of something that is good in itself: being alive. He concludes his essay by writing that, "If there is no limit to the amount of life that it would be good to have, then it may be that a bad end is in store for us all" (1991: 10).

Williams takes this to be an argument in favour of immortality, and therefore flawed. One can see how Nagel's view might be taken this way. If more life is better than less, it is better just to keep living than to die at any moment. But to keep living is to be immortal. So immortality is better than mortality.

However, Nagel does not discuss immortality explicitly. This turns out to be an important point. Near the beginning of this chapter, we distinguished two possible types of human immortality: immortality where one recognizes that one is immortal, and immortality without that recognition. We saw that if we are to imagine ourselves as human beings, the only immortality we could reasonably consider was immortality with recognition. That, in turn, has a number of consequences, most of them negative, in its impact on our lives. In our distinction between the way immortality threatens the meaningfulness of human life internally and externally, all of the internal threats require realizing that one is immortal. The gloominess that Borges depicts and the lack of seriousness discussed by Nussbaum require that immortal beings understand themselves to be immortal.

The external threat to meaningfulness, that life just keeps going on, also requires recognition of one's immortality. The boredom and despair that overtake one are a result of the realization that there is still more living left and nothing of interest or passion to fill it. It is possible, of course, that one could not recognize that one was immortal. In that case, the internal threat to meaninglessness would not exist, and one might keep the external threat at bay, at least for a while. However, as we saw, this would not be a *human* life, and what we're interested in is a human life that would be immortal. That is what helps us understand our relation to death.

The fact that Nagel does not explicitly discuss this allows us to see his argument in a different light from the way Williams sees it. We might say that Nagel's view is not that people should be immortal, but that they should keep on living. This distinction may seem strange. It may seem like what philosophers call a distinction without a difference: a distinction where the things distinguished are actually the same. Human immortality is immortality with the recognition that one is immortal. This is not what Nagel argues for. His view is that death, whenever it comes, is bad for us. To put the point another way, Nagel argues that, from the perspective of a mortal being, death is always an evil. He does not argue that, from the perspective of a mortal being, immortality would be good. Nor does he argue, and this is the crucial point, that from the perspective of an immortal being immortality is a good thing. He just doesn't consider those possibilities.

Now one might want to say that it doesn't matter whether he considers those possibilities or not; they still follow from what he has said. This seems to be Williams's view when he writes:

> death is at any time an evil ... Nagel, indeed, from his point of view, does seem to permit that conclusion ... But wider consequences follow. For if all that is true, then it looks as though it would be not only always better to live, but better to live always, that is, never to die.   (1976: 89)

But do those wider consequences necessarily follow? Might there be a way of thinking about death such that, in one sense, it is better to keep living while, in another sense, it is better not to be immortal? That is the dilemma this chapter has been building towards. If death is an evil, so is immortality, although in a different way.

Williams does not see a dilemma here. He recognizes immortality as an evil, for reasons we have seen throughout this chapter. His conclusion, then, is that mortality is not an evil. It's all a question of timing. One must just live long enough that one's passion for living remains intact. Less than that and one dies prematurely: longer than that and one dies bored with life. This, of course, is easier said than done. It's not even clear that most humans are allotted the proper amount of time to avoid premature death. But there is, in Williams's view a proper time for each life, even if it is an elusive matter to know when that time is. He writes of death that:

> Necessarily, it tends to be either too early or too late. EM [Elina Makropoulos, the fictional immortal character] reminds us that it can be too late, and many, as against Lucretius, need no reminding that it can be too early. If that is any sort of dilemma, it can, as things still are and if one is exceptionally lucky, be resolved, not by doing anything, but just by dying shortly before the horrors of not doing so become evident.
>
> (*Ibid.*: 100)

The key phrase in this passage is *shortly before*. If one dies shortly before the horrors of not dying become evident, then one has died too soon. Life, at that point, continues to be valuable. One is attached to one's living, if only to the type of bare experience Nagel discusses. Now one might argue that perhaps there is a moment, right after everything worth living for is gone and right before the horrors of living too long become evident, that would be the perfect moment to die. It seems to me that this is a possibility – in fact, we recognized that possibility in Chapter 1 – but a very unlikely one. For most of us, our attachments to life do not cease altogether in some orchestrated way at a particular moment that would then be the perfect moment to die. Rather, there are, in the metaphor we have been appealing to often, always threads that bind us to the world. The idea that those threads would come together at a particular moment right before everything would turn bad seems remote.

If this is right, then the idea that there is a right time to die is less plausible, at least for the overwhelming majority, the near unanimity, of human lives. Williams, in arguing against immortality, has tipped the boat a bit too far in the other direction. It may be that while immortality would be a bad option for us, so is dying. It may be, as Nagel has argued, that a bad end is in store for us all. If we see things this way, then Nagel's position can appear to be somewhat more nuanced than the logical formulation Williams gives it: dying is bad at any moment, therefore immortality is good. We can take Nagel to be arguing, not that immortality is good, but that for most of us dying at any particular moment is bad. This begins to capture the dilemma death presents to us. It is better that we are mortal creatures, but there is no good time to die. Our mortality brings our lives shape; it gives those lives coherence and meaning. It makes the moments of those lives precious. And yet, dying threatens all that as well. It is good that we die, but never just yet.

Of course, this *never just yet* will not hold for everyone. For some people, those in great emotional or physical pain, particularly those who suffer illnesses that are at once debilitating and terminal, it might be better to die sooner rather than later. But even for many of them, the fact that they will die plays a role in their decision to die sooner. For them, there is no future in which to project their lives. It is not just a matter of living in great pain, but of living in such pain with no opportunity to engage in the kinds of projects that make a human life meaningful. There is not enough time left for those projects. The existence of a future offers hope. The prospect of living a short time in great pain and then dying does not.

There is a larger lesson here. One might want to counter the dilemma I have brought forward here by noting that many people who have lived long and satisfying lives, when they come to the end of those lives, are ready to die. They make peace with death. For them, is there not a right time to die? Wouldn't Williams then be right, at least in a not negligible number of cases?

The problem with this example is that the people in question know they are going to die, and so what they make peace with is inevitability. These people have not been offered the choice of living more and dying. Rather, they see themselves coming to the end of their lives, they know that their time is nearly done, and they have the emotional resources to come to terms with that fact. They do not seek to die. They face with equanimity a dying they cannot avoid. For people like this, the prospect of more living would probably be embraced. But since that is not on the cards, they accept what is.

This does not mean that there is nobody who is not terminally ill who would ever want to die. One might point to people who commit suicide. This, though, does not provide much evidence against the idea that death is an evil for us. Recent research has found that the vast majority of potential suicides, if thwarted in their attempt, do not try it again. Suicide seems mostly to find its source in temporary desperation rather than reasonable reflection on the state of one's life. But, within the population of people who attempt suicide, there are those who repeat the attempt if given the opportunity. They are very few, but they exist. Sad as it is, there are people whose lives are such sources of pain that for them to keep on living would be a burden to them. For whatever reasons, their lives have lost what meaning they once had, and it is unlikely that meaning will return to them. These people are not caught in the dilemma we are discussing here. However, their situation is worse than the dilemma whose contours we are following.

What is that dilemma? That both death and immortality are inimical to us. If death is a bad end for us all, immortality would be a bad lack of end for us all. This dilemma, which is perhaps the most important dilemma facing human beings, is not the kind of thing one resolves theoretically. It is not a puzzle that one thinks one's way through to a resolution. It is a dilemma that each of us faces in our living, a dilemma that structures how we go about creating ourselves. The death that haunts us is that which allows our lives to have significance to us.

The question each of our lives faces is how to live in the face of this dilemma. What do we make of ourselves if the death that undermines us is a necessary feature of our lives being worthwhile? At the outset, we must recognize that it cannot be a question of resolving the dilemma. Williams tries to resolve it in one direction: in favour of death. Nagel, at least on Williams's reading, tries to resolve it in the other direction. We have seen here, however, that there is no resolution. It is not a question of solving the problem death places before us, but of figuring out how to live with it. Of course, there are many different ways of navigating this dilemma. There is no single formula to which all lives must conform. But there are some general considerations we can bring to bear on the problem, and to these we now turn.

3. Living with death

Let us take stock of where we are. In asking about death, we have been asking about it as a finality: as a definitive end to a life. We want to understand what this might mean for each of us in his or her living. If death is not final, it is not really death. As we have put it, an afterlife allows us to survive our own death. Some part of you may die, but *you* don't really die.

What if you do die? What if there is nothing left of you after your heart stops beating and your brainwaves go flat? Then death is simply the stoppage of life. It is not its conclusion in any way other than being the point at which you stop living. Moreover, that stoppage could happen at any moment. All that is certain is that it will happen. The curtain will come down on your life, and it could do so in the middle of the play. You always see the curtain there, hovering above you. You may live so that it is less likely that the curtain will come down sooner rather than later. You may eat well, exercise, drive cautiously. This lowers the probably of the curtain just dropping on you unexpectedly. But it does not eliminate the very possibility of its coming down. Genetic predispositions, natural disasters, bad drivers who share the road with you: all of these tug at the curtains of people's lives.

The haunting fear of death could make one long for immortality. At least with immortality there is no fear of the curtain coming down on some important scene or another of your life. However, immortality brings its own problems. A play that goes on and on is boring, and if you know going in (or soon after it starts) that the play of your life will go on without ceasing you're likely to become bored with it. No particular part of it will matter. None of it will have any significance or urgency. Relationships will probably be shallower, commitments looser, and time will hang heavy at every moment. There will be no place to hide from the endlessness of your own existence. Your projects will eventually run out of steam or passion, and you will know this as you engage in them. Your unfolding experience will not have the wonder it does for mortal creatures, since it will always be there. And even if you seek refuge in pure thought or speculation, you will lose interest in it, since it will not have a life – your life – as its wellspring.

It is no wonder that so many of us avoid confronting death. It is like a disease whose cure, if it existed, would be worse than the disease itself. Of course, the simplest and most common way to avoid the spectre of death is simply not to think about it. It's akin to that slight grinding noise that you hear in the car. Maybe if you ignore it then it will just go away. The opposite tack, though, is no better. Constant reflection on death is no better a strategy than ignoring it. This is because constant reflection on death is usually an attempt to cure it or control it. But death cannot be cured or controlled. Staring up at the curtain will not prevent it from falling. To be perpetually thinking about death in an attempt to ward off its danger is to be like obsessive-compulsive people who cannot stop washing their hands. They feel continuously threatened by dirt or impurity, so they hope that with enough cleansing they will keep them at bay. But germs, and death, will always be with us. There is no ritual that eliminates them or even ensures that we have any space between us and them.

When ignoring death (or, its opposite, obsessing about death) won't do, the next most common strategy is to think about death in a way that circumvents it. This, as we have seen, is what an afterlife does. It avoids death by keeping one's essence intact after one's physical demise. In the examples we have studied, some versions of

Christianity and Buddhism both do this, although in very different ways. There is a very different case, that of Taoism, that provides an interesting contrast to both Christianity and Buddhism. We can only gesture at that contrast momentarily, but it might be worth pausing to see it at work.

In Taoism, as in Buddhism, there is a cycle of life and death. But there is no karma. Each of us is like a wave on the sea of being. We arise from the sea, thinking ourselves to be unique and irreplaceable individuals only because we don't see that we are nothing more than temporary movements of something larger. Eventually, we will return to that larger something and become a part of it. Taoism, like Buddhism, takes the concept of the self to be illusory. There is simply the unfolding process of the cosmos, and what appears to be a self is nothing more than a moment in that cosmic unfolding. But, unlike those Buddhists who believe in reincarnation, Taoism is more consistent in this regard. Reincarnation has implicit in it the idea of a self. That self may disappear again when it reaches nirvana, but at least it remains throughout a series of lives. Taoism possesses no concept like this. One is born, one dies, one returns to the cosmic source from whence one came and that, in reality, one never left.

How is death conceived in Taoism? This is a bit unclear. From one perspective, one surely dies. There is nothing left of one after the wave falls back into the sea. Of course, the idea of there being someone, a self, that dies is itself mistaken. But that aside, in as much as there is an experience of self, it ends with one's death. Conceived this way, Taoism does not have a concept of the afterlife. The themes of death we isolated in Chapter 1 remain intact.

However, there is another perspective that complicates matters. In some ways of speaking, after one's death one returns to the cosmic stuff, but does not entirely disappear. In the writings of the ancient Taoist Chuang Tzu, for instance, a character celebrates his impending death, seeing it as a chance for further adventures. He wonders what the various parts of him will become next. What the character calls the Creator:

> will perhaps in time ... transform my left arm into a rooster ... Or perhaps he'll transform my right arm into a crossbow pellet and I'll shoot down an owl for roasting. Or perhaps in time he'll transform my buttocks into cartwheels. Then, with my spirit for a horse, I'll climb up and go for a ride.
>
> (1964: 80–81)

Taken this way, there is a sense, albeit an unusual one, in which one does survive one's own death. One is dispersed back into the cosmic stuff, to be sure. But there is more left for one to experience. It may be in diverse places and forms, but there is something to look forward to. This perspective would provide an afterlife, if one very different from those envisaged by Christianity or Buddhism.

One could give some empirical backing to the Taoist idea, but perhaps at the expense of any comfort in the face of death that it would offer. For if we think of ecological systems, we can recognize that we are indeed part of those systems. Currently, the effects of global warming are reminding us of this. So if we consider ourselves as biological matter, then our deaths return us to the soil. We nourish the soil, which then becomes part of plant matter (assuming we do not close ourselves off in a coffin). Plants are eaten by animals, and then become part of their biological makeup. In this way, our biological dispersion does in fact become, in a sense, rooster legs and crossbow pellets and cartwheels (although the latter two not so much any more). However, seen this way, we still die. What is important to us about our lives is extinguished. Therefore, unless this perspective helps remove us from the meaningfulness of our engagements (which, in fact, Taoism does seek to do – a point we shall return to shortly), then it does not help us elude the haunting power of death.

In addition to not thinking about death, obsessing over it and embracing the concept of an afterlife, we have seen at least one other strategy to escape death's grip. This is Bernard Williams's claim that it is at least possible to die at the right time. This way of thinking about death does not deny or neglect the fact that people die. What it denies, at least sometimes, is the second theme associated with death: that death is not a goal or an accomplishment. We should be clear here, so we don't misrepresent Williams's position. He does not say that death comes at the right time for many or most of us. He says that it is possible that death could come at the right time: that moment right before our lives descend into the boredom associated with immortality. Perhaps that moment would take a lot longer to arrive than a human life actually lasts. He does not deny that possibility. He thinks only that there could be a moment like that for human lives. And that is the source of a certain hope associated with one's death: the hope that death can be a proper ending to a life.

From the perspective we have been building here, that hope would be diminished. It is, perhaps, not impossible that death could come at the right time. In the previous chapter, we discussed some exceptional circumstances in which death might be timely. However, given the way humans engage in projects, given how we orient ourselves towards the future, it is difficult to see how death could arrive at an appropriate time for most of us. Perhaps if humans lived a couple of hundred years, the situation might be different. But we don't. Given the life spans of human beings, and except for situations in which a life is going poorly with no prospects for improvement, it is unlikely that death could come at the right moment for any of us.

There is yet another strategy for eluding the power of death. It is one we have not discussed. And yet, many people refer to it in one way or another. When they do, they see it as a sort of immortality. It involves the goal of leaving one's mark on the world, impressing upon the world something lasting that could maintain one's influence, or even one's name, beyond the grave. This can be sought through grand and expensive gestures: donating money for a wing of a hospital or a college building. It can be sought – yes indeed – through the writing of a book. It can even be sought through having children, whom I have heard referred to more than once as a "bid for immortality". The idea in all these cases is that one leaves something of oneself behind. One tries to assure oneself that there is a remainder in this world after one has left it.

How does this assurance work? It is obviously of no use to one after one has died. If I have a building erected in my name, I will not know about this building after my death. It will give me no solace then. It can operate only as an assurance for the living. I donate money for a building that will bear my name, telling myself that after I die I will be remembered. And in that memory I will live on. This does not have to be my only motive for donating money for a building. For those who donate – or write books, or have children – it may not be a motive at all. But for those for whom it is a motive, it probably works as a consolation to the living while they are alive.

It is a small consolation, though, in the face of death. First, these stabs at keeping one's name or influence alive do not succeed in keeping one's experience alive. I die, and no building bearing my name can stop that. I will no longer awake to see the leaves against the sky, or feel my wife next to me, or hear my kids' voices. My writing will cease. My hopes for and my engagements with this world will come to an end with me. In short, leaving something behind does not leave *me* behind. In as much as such actions are a bid for immortality, then, they serve only as a poor substitute.

Secondly, the immortality these acts confer becomes thinner with the years. There are those who remember me, and in whose memory I continue to live when they enter the building I have funded or meet my children or read my books. But they will die too, and the next generation will know of me only through the stories told to them by those who knew me. Those stories will probably not be very important to them, and so they will be forgotten by the next generation. If I'm lucky a fact or two about my life will still be associated with my gesture toward immortality. In a few generations, though, there will be only some yellowed books with my name on the spine, or a building bearing a name nobody recognizes, or great grandchildren for whom I am only a place on a family tree, if that. Marcus Aurelius recognizes this clearly. In his *Meditations*, he writes:

> All things fade into the storied past, and in a little while are shrouded in oblivion. Even to men whose lives were a blaze of glory this comes to pass; as for the rest, the breath is hardly out of them before, in Homer's words, they are "lost to sight alike and hearsay".   (Bk 4, §33)

What do all these approaches to death have in common? What binds the neglect of death, constant reflection on death, the embrace of an afterlife, the idea that death can come at the right moment, and the attempt to leave an indelible mark on the world? I would like to put it this way: in one way or another, they all neglect the *fragility* of life. If we are to come to terms with the dilemma we found ourselves in at the end of the previous chapter, it is this fragility we must recognize and learn to live with, and to live within.

In appealing to the fragility of life I am not adding anything to what we have already said. Instead, it is a way of summing up the previous themes. Human life is vulnerable to death. It can be broken by death at any time. Because of this, it is fragile not only at the end of but throughout its existence. At the same time, this fragility makes it valuable in a way that it would not be if it were not fragile. We take care of it, we look after it, we concern ourselves with it in ways that we would not were it not fragile.

Consider an object such as an antique watch. Suppose you owned one, something passed down the generations. You could put it away

85

in a drawer or display it in a glass case or on a mantelpiece. That would protect the watch, but at a cost. In a sense, it would not be a watch any more. It would be a museum piece, and the fact that it told time would be irrelevant to it. It would not matter whether it still had its inside workings, except maybe for you to be able to boast that it could keep time, or maybe carefully open it up to display its workings, and then put it back in the case or on the shelf. It would no longer be a watch; it would be art, in the sterile sense in which we often use the term. (Think here of how sterile most art looks in museums or galleries. It seems out of context, hung on walls or displayed on pedestals in rooms that have no purpose other than to show it to the public. There is no integration of this art into human life, and it shows. It feels removed in a way that it wouldn't in someone's living room or in an office.)

Of course, you wouldn't have to treat your watch in that way. You could go in the opposite direction, and treat it like nothing more than a practical object. It's a watch; it tells the time. You slap it on your wrist before you go to work, and throw it among your work clothes at the end of the day. Treating it this way at least allows it to function according to its purpose. The problem is, if you treat an antique watch too cavalierly, it will not function as a watch for very long. Using a watch as a watch is great, but there does seem to be something not quite right about treating an antique watch like a Timex. It seems to deserve better than that, because it's a valuable and fragile object. You break a Timex, and you just order another. You break this watch and you're out of luck.

Probably the best way to treat the watch, then, is to wear it, but to be careful: not neurotically careful, but careful in the way of enjoying it without abusing it, keeping in the back of your mind the fact that you have it on, and perhaps every once in a while looking at it and allowing its beauty or its age or its character to impress you. There isn't a single right way to do this. What moves you about wearing an old family watch may be different from what moves me.

Each of us wears the watch in his or her own way. But each of us wears it, and each of us tries to keep it from unnecessary harm.

This does not mean that nothing will happen to your watch. You could get caught in a rainstorm or forget about it and stick your wrist under a tap. The band could break. Somebody could steal it when you take it off and lay it aside. None of these, though, would justify your keeping it on the mantelpiece or in a glass case. Better to wear it for a short time than not at all.

The analogy here, of course, is with a human life in the face of death. We have to think about how to live, recognizing that we will die. This does not lead us to a mindless self-preservation that seeks to keep us alive at all costs. Nor does it lead us to ignoring the possibility of death. The first seeks an immortality it would be better not to have. The second acts as though we were immortal, or alternatively embraces death at the expense of life. Neither of these recognizes that human life is fragile, that it is always exposed to death. To be exposed to death is not to be dying, but rather to live in the face of one's inevitable and uncertain death. We must ask what it is to do this, how it is that one might live a fragile life.

There are many ways. We shall focus on living the fragility itself, which is equivalent to living the dilemma that neither death nor immortality is good for us, or, otherwise put, that death is both a central source of and a central threat to life's meaning. The question will be one of how to think about our lives in the shadow cast both by death and by this dilemma. However, before we turn there we should linger over an approach to living that recognizes the fragility of life without asking how one might live within it. This approach works by stepping back from the fragility of human life and places it within a larger picture. Placed within the larger picture, we perhaps loosen our grip on life, which makes death less threatening. We see our lives, fragile as they are, as less important than we make them out to be. And if our lives are less important, then our death will be less important as well.

One way of taking this approach is offered by the ancient Epicurean philosopher Lucretius. Lucretius has a number of arguments against the harm of death. One of them, borrowed directly from Epicurus, we have already seen. It is the argument that since we are not there to experience death, death is nothing to us. Another of Lucretius's arguments, which we will not take up here, is that since we are not upset about the fact that things were going on before our birth, we should not be upset about them going on after our death. This argument has been called the symmetry argument by later philosophers, since it sees a symmetry between the *before* and the *after* of our lives. The argument of concern to us does not say that we ought not to be concerned about our death, or be attached to life, or think of our death as nothing to us; rather, it concerns other people.

There are people being born all the time. If nobody died, then the world would grow overcrowded. In our time, as opposed to Lucretius's, it is already overcrowded. Imagine what it would be like if nobody died. Everyone's life would be worse. After a certain point, each new person being born into the world could look forward to nothing more than a deeply competitive existence for the few resources and little space there would be on the planet. In fairness, then, everyone should have a chance at a decent life rather than a life in crowded and harsh conditions. The only way to make this happen is for everyone to have a turn. When your turn is over, it's time to leave turns for the people who follow. Death ensures that everyone has a turn. It may not be a fair turn: some people's lives are shorter than others, and many people's lives go worse than others through no fault of their own. Death does not cure all problems of fairness. But at least it cures one, by making sure that everyone allows everyone else a turn. Death is like passing the baton on to the next generation.

One might want to object to Lucretius here by saying that it is a bit abstract to speak of turns belonging to people who don't exist yet. If there were only the people who currently exist who were immortal, then there would be no unfairness. Unfairness only happens because people are being born. But many people who will be born are not yet even conceived. What unfairness can there be to them if nobody dies? There isn't even a *them* to be unfair to. Who are our children before we meet those with whom we become parents? They are nobody, and there is no such thing as an unfairness to nobody.

There are a couple of problems with this objection. First, we do in fact give birth. So to make the objection compelling, we would have to posit a world of immortality without birth. That raises all the problems with immortality we saw in the previous chapter. Secondly, given that we do give birth, there are always people around to whom it would be increasingly unfair if we were immortal. We can think of it this way. Children who are being born now are coming into a world that already has a strain on its resources. If those of us who are currently alive didn't die, that strain would only increase. It would be difficult for those children as they grew older. Plus, they might be reluctant to have their own children because of the extra strain it would place on the limited available resources. So there are people alive today to whom it would be unfair if the rest of us did not make room. And this unfairness would only increase with each generation.

Lucretius's argument, then, is that fairness dictates that each of us takes his or her turn at life and then passes it to those who have not yet had a turn, or at least a full turn. This argument is very different from the kinds of arguments we've seen so far. It does not concern how well or badly your or my life goes. It is not an issue of what death does or does not do to you or me. Rather, it concerns the effect of your and my death on other people. It does not say that death is good for the person who dies. It says that death is good for those who are left. Or, more specifically, it says that death is good so that the next generation of those who are left have a shot at living decently. In terms sometimes invoked by philosophers, this argument is not self-regarding but other-regarding.

So far in this book we have immersed ourselves in self-regarding reflections about death. This is our focus, since our question is one of how to live with the fact that one will die. Lucretius's argument turns our attention away from ourselves and towards others who need access to the planet's resources. One might think, then, that it does not have a bearing on the question that drives us. But it does, although indirectly. Recognizing the unfairness of immortality might allow me to step a little away from my own life. In particular, it might allow me to step away from the attachment to my life in favour of allowing others to live a fuller life. It might allow me to recognize that I'm not the only one attached to my life, and that perhaps I should diminish, or at least take some perspective on, my own attachment in the face of the needs of others. In this way, it does address the question of how to live in the face of one's own death.

It does this by placing my own death in a larger perspective. Rather than being alone with my death, I am instead one person among others whose death fits into a larger pattern of living and dying. My death comes to have a meaning, a purpose, within this larger pattern. The purpose it has is very different from any sense of accomplishment or goal that we denied to death in Chapter 1. There it was a question of death giving my life meaning. Here it is an issue of death having meaning by clearing the way for the lives of others. Death still accomplishes nothing for me. But it does accomplish something for others, by letting them have a fuller turn at life.

Another way to step back from the fragility of life without denying that fragility comes with Taoist philosophy. Taoism shares with Lucretius's argument the goal of placing one's own life and death within a larger pattern. This pattern, however, is different from the one Lucretius focuses on. We have already seen that the Taoist view of the self after death can be taken in at least two ways.

If a human life is a wave in the sea of being, then it would seem that there is nothing left of the self that occupied that life after the wave falls back into the sea. However, sometimes Taoists speak as though something of oneself remains, but in a dispersed way. That second way would deny, at least after a fashion, that one's self actually ends with one's death. Let's look at the first way, however. That's the way for which we gave the ecological example. In this way of taking up Taoism, one's death returns one to the larger cosmic stuff from which one emerged – and which, really, one never left. This view retains the fragility of life that we have insisted on here. Death haunts a human life. It is not an accomplishment or a goal but only an ending. There is nothing of oneself left after death. Where, then, is the solace lent to mortal creatures aware of their impending death?

It lies in what happens before one is born and especially after one dies. There is, for Taoism, a larger whole of which one is a part, whether living or dead. One has a place in a cosmic process of which one's own existence is a fleeting moment, but a moment nonetheless. The process itself has no goal or meaning, any more than an ecosystem can be said to have a goal or a meaning. However, one is still part of that process, and even when one dies the process continues with one's material remains.

Here is an analogy. When people join a political demonstration or are part of the audience at an important sports event, they often feel like a part of something bigger than themselves. Their own individual significance loses some of its hold on them. That is why, for instance, people are often more willing to sacrifice their time and effort as a part of a political campaign than they would normally be willing to do. (This is less so at sporting events.) When someone feels to be a part of a larger whole, the whole gains in significance while he or she, as a part, begins to see himself or herself as drawing significance from participation in that whole. Taoism offers a similar experience but on a cosmic scale. One's life and death is part of the process of the universe in its unfolding. To be a part of that process while one lives, and to remain within that process when one dies, may give one's life a sense of meaning and one's death an appropriate place, even if the process itself does not ultimately have a meaning outside itself.

This is not to say that Taoism necessarily does this for everyone. There are those for whom the place in the larger whole does not confer meaningfulness or consolation. The loss of one's self is not compensated for by the process of which one is a part. There are others who will insist that without the process having any ultimate meaning, one's place in it will not have meaning either. In contrast to Lucretius's argument, one's death does not gain any meaning through its contribution to the lives of other people. Some may find that lack of contribution to be a bar to embracing the Taoist perspective. The reason I raise the example of Taoism is that, like Lucretius's argument, it does not deny that life is fragile, but seeks instead to place that fragility within a larger viewpoint from which it loses its grip on us.

Both of these perspectives diverge from the several ways of seeking to escape fragility that we canvassed earlier in this chapter. Compare, for example, Lucretius's argument with the view that we have an afterlife. In the latter case, we actually survive our death. For Lucretius, we do not survive our death. We remain exposed to death throughout our lives in the ways described in Chapter 1. Life is fragile, lived always in the face of death. However, when death comes, it will at least be a benefit to others. In contrast to views that embrace an afterlife, there will be nothing of us left after death. However, that death, although bereft of significance for our lives, will be a benefit to others. And, indirectly, that may be a consolation to us.

Again, compare the Taoist viewpoint with Williams's view that there may be a right time to die. A right time to die would give a sense of wholeness to one's own life. It would round out a life, bring it to its proper conclusion. Taoism does not concern itself with the wholeness or conclusion of one's life. One's life and one's self do not matter at all to the cosmic process whence one came and to which one will return. It is only when one steps back from the concerns of one's own life that Taoism offers its riches. Death does not confer meaning or place to a life. It is the place of life and death in the process that confers meaning.

Both Lucretius's argument and Taoism are compatible with the fragility of life. Unlike the other perspectives, they do not seek to deny or to escape the character of that fragility. The reason they do so is that they ask us to take that fragility less seriously in the name of something else. For Lucretius, that something else is the lives of others; for Taoism, it is the process behind and within life. This movement away from the fragility of life has another implication. If neither perspective denies the fragility of life it is because neither of them engages it. They do not ask what it is to live a fragile life. That is not their concern. Instead they ask how we might think of things so that fragility becomes less pressing to us.

If the approach common to both perspectives – stepping back from life's fragility – does not deny that fragility, nor does it immerse itself within the difficulties fragility brings. We might think of that approach as operating with this message: yes, life is stalked by a death that has no point or meaning, and yes, immortality would be worse, but looked at from a larger perspective these things matter less than they seem to. This may be an important message to some, and I don't want to deny its potential power. If this approach, either in the form of Lucretius's argument (but not his whole philosophy, which goes in a different direction) or Taoism, or in some other form, is embraced, it can blunt the power of death over us. However, it does not answer – and does not seek to answer – the question that occupies us here: how do we live from *within* the perspective of a fragile life? Regardless of what might happen to us afterwards, and regardless of how our death affects others, how can each of us live knowing, as Nagel has put it, that "there is a bad end in store for us all"? *Can* we live knowing this? Must we somehow navigate around this knowledge, either by some form of escape or by putting it into a perspective in which it loses some of its sting?

First, let us make sure we're clear about what we're asking. The question is not one of whether we can live within life's fragility. If the perspective we have been building so far is right, then not only can we, but we must. The fragility of life is simply where we are. Our lives are conducted in the face of a death, which, if we can put it this way, is the source of both their meaning and their meaning-lessness. It is the source of their meaning for reasons we saw in Chapter 2 regarding immortality, and the source of meaningless-ness for reasons we saw in Chapter 1. Whether we can live fragile lives is not the question: the fragility of life is our situation.

The question is whether we can live with the knowledge of this. And even here we need to be more precise. In some sense, we can always live with the knowledge of the fragility of life. You might come away from this book convinced by the first two chapters that neither death nor immortality offers us what a human life would want. You might say to yourself, "Yes, that's right: death both gives and takes away meaning in a human life". And then you might go on as though none of this mattered. You forget it, not in your beliefs but in your life. If someone asked you whether life was fragile in the way this book describes, you'd affirm it. But it wouldn't affect you. It would be a snippet of knowledge like lots of other snippets of know-ledge you have. It would have no more bearing on your life than knowing that the earth is ninety-three million miles from the sun.

The issue before us is different. It is whether we can live, not within the fragility of life, nor in the knowledge that life is fragile, but *within* the knowledge that life is fragile. Can that knowledge have an impact in our thinking about our life? Can we live according to this knowledge? If my claim at the outset of the book is right – that death is the most important fact about us – then knowing the role death plays in our lives would seem to be significant in thinking about how to live. Can we integrate that knowledge into our lives? That is the question we're pursuing here.

There might be a temptation to say that we cannot live this way, because the fragility of life is a contradiction, and one cannot live a contradiction. If death both gives and withdraws meaningfulness in life, then we would have to live both sides of this, which is impossible. We need to resist this temptation at the outset. First, it is unclear whether people can or cannot live a contradiction. It's often said in philosophy that one cannot *believe* a contradiction, or at least that one cannot coherently believe one. I cannot coherently believe both that the sky is blue and that the sky is not blue. Fair enough. But living is not the same thing as believing. It is possible that people might live contradictions they cannot believe. One of the tasks of psychotherapy is to bring to light contradictions that people live in order to allow people to confront them. Now one might say here that these lives are not coherently lived, and that may be. But the incoherence of a life is not the same thing as the incoherence of a belief. It is a more complicated affair than believing and disbelieving something at the same time.

However, the exact character of living a contradiction need not detain us, because the fragility of life does not involve a contradiction. It involves a difficulty, one that can be put paradoxically, but not a contradiction. If we say that death is the source both of the meaningfulness and meaninglessness of life, we are not giving voice to some kind of contradictory statement. The way in which death bestows meaning on life and the way it withdraws it are different. Death bestows meaning on life because it offers it the possibility of having a shape that immortality would deny. It also gives life's moments a preciousness and urgency that would go lacking if living went on without end. At the same time, the fact that death is a constant companion, if not in fact at least in possibility, puts our relationships and our commitments at constant risk

95

and assures us that at the end they will not form a whole or lead us to a goal that will lend our lives an ultimate significance. Death may give a human life shape, but at the cost of wholeness. It may allow for passion, but at the cost of putting the meaning of that passion at risk.

There are subtleties here, which we have followed throughout the course of this book. But the fragility of life offers no contradiction, either to belief or to life itself.

Even if there is no contradiction here, that does not assure us that we can live within the fragility of life. There are many ways that living in accordance with something can be impossible. A purported contradiction would be only one of them. (And, as we have seen, it might not even be one.) It could be that it is just too hard to live this way. Facing death and the difficulties it brings might be beyond the powers of a human being. It might be emotionally overwhelming. Or, at the other end of the spectrum, it could be that the fragility of life has nothing to teach us. It could be that there is nothing more to do here than to acknowledge death's power and move on. I suspect few readers will be tempted by this option, and nor am I. But if there is something to be learned, something about the fragility of life that we can live within, what is it?

There is surely a multitude of ways to approach this question. I would like to do so by starting with an ancient philosopher, one who seems to me to have part of the truth. We can follow his thought as far as it leads us, and then continue it from there in order to see how living within fragility might be possible. The philosopher Marcus Aurelius became convinced by the doctrine of Stoicism, and dedicated himself to living in accordance with what he saw as its dictates. Stoicism is a complex doctrine, involving questions not only of living but also of science and of logic. We need not linger over the larger framework of Stoicism, except in as much as it has a bearing on Aurelius's search to face his life and his death in a Stoical manner.

Aurelius's attempt to live Stoically is expressed in his *Meditations*, from which we have already drawn a quote. We should be clear what the *Meditations* are, however, since it is easy to misread them. I have had students tell me that they have read Aurelius and found him to be both preachy and repetitive. And, if one reads the *Meditations* as a set of lectures, that's exactly how it comes off. There are repetitive exhortations about what one ought to do and how one ought to live and why one is never doing these things. The trick in reading the *Meditations*, though, is to know that they are not lectures. They are reflective writings Aurelius penned in order to grapple with his life. They were not meant for publication, or to be read by others. They are, in short, a documentation of one man's struggle with himself to live more in accordance with what he believed. The French historian of ancient philosophy Pierre Hadot has called them *spiritual exercises*.

What is a spiritual exercise? It is a certain type of mental exercise. We do exercises like them every day, usually when we tell ourselves to prepare for something we need to do or tolerate or undergo. Before an important presentation, people often envisage it; they see themselves giving the presentation, making the particular points, standing in front of a group of people. When I was preparing to run mile races, I would often envisage each lap, actually trying to see myself run. The idea behind these types of mental exercises is that they ready a person for what is about to come. Doing them is like putting on a certain mental armour or girding one's emotional loins. Then, when faced with the difficulties of the presentation or the run or whatever, one is not taken by surprise. Yes, one tells oneself, here is what I expected.

A spiritual exercise is a mental exercise of a particular kind. It seeks to prepare one to live as one thinks one ought to in the face of whatever distractions and temptations the world offers. "Begin each day", Aurelius writes, "by telling yourself: Today I shall be meeting with interference, ingratitude, insolence, disloyalty, ill-will, and selfishness – all of them due to the offenders' ignorance of what is good or evil" (Book 2, §1). As a Stoic, Aurelius does not want to be driven by other people's behaviours. He wants to remain at peace with himself. So he tells himself to prepare for those things that are likely to remove that peace.

Many ancient philosophers engaged in spiritual exercises. Especially in the morning, before the day began, and again at night as a sort of spiritual assessment of their day, they would remind themselves of what was important, how they sought to live, what might stand in their way and how they should deal with it. Spiritual exercises are a kind of envisaging of one's daily life, but within the framework of a larger philosophical perspective.

Aurelius's *Meditations* are the record of a set of spiritual exercises. They are perhaps the best record that has come down to us. They show us a man at work on himself: seeking to make himself better than he is, more Stoical. Seen this way, the exhortations that characterize the *Meditations* are not preachy advice given to others, but expressions of a man struggling with himself, and often seeing himself as a failure. It's as though he often said to himself: you knew what was important yesterday and yet you will not live up to it today: "Think of your many years of procrastination; how the gods have repeatedly granted you further periods of grace, of which you have taken no advantage" (Book 2, §4).

Much of what Aurelius writes to himself concerns death. He brings death to bear in trying to get himself to live as he ought to. Often, he enlists death to help him live in accordance with the Stoic belief that only the present exists. The future is not yet and the past is no longer. One must live fully in the present. Meditating on death promotes this recognition in at least two ways, both of which involve limiting one's concern about the future. First, as we have seen, death can come at any time. Since the future does not exist, nothing of it is guaranteed. We may have years to live, and we may have only a day. So we cannot live with expectations about the future. We can only make the present our duty. We must live well now, without concern for a future whose shape and existence is unclear to us.

The Stoics embedded this belief in another one that many of us are no longer tempted to hold. It is the belief that the universe is basically rational, that everything happens for a reasonable purpose. Of course, we sometimes say to ourselves that "everything happens for a reason", and this colloquialism is close to the Stoic doctrine of an essentially benign universe. However, it is unclear that when we say it we mean it as literally as the Stoics did. It is often more likely a saying or a vague hope among us, not a philosophical doctrine of the kind the Stoics held.

Do we need to hold this doctrine in order to follow Aurelius's emphasis on the present? I don't think so. His concern with the present can grip us even in the absence of a trust in the ultimate rationality of the universe. His point is not that if we take care of the present, everything in the future will work out. It is rather that *there is no future*: there is only the present. We cannot live in something that does not exist or that we cannot control. Whether, as the Stoics believed, that which we cannot control is ultimately rational, or whether we believe that the universe is contingent or arbitrary, we can still embrace the Stoic belief that only the present exists. That is the heart of the first role death plays in Aurelius's meditations.

The second role that death plays for him is to remind us of how soon each of us is forgotten. We do much to impress ourselves upon the world, to make ourselves remembered, to imprint our existence. And yet, as Aurelius often reminds himself, after we die we are quickly forgotten. Our legacy is short in the larger span of history. "All of us", he reminds himself, "are creatures of a day; the remem-berer and the remembered alike" (Book 4, §35). One can imagine that it would be a difficult task for a Roman emperor to be humble in this regard; there would be a strong temptation to think that one's decisions and actions would have consequences stretching far into the future. It would be no easy thing for Aurelius to bear in mind the limitations of his own life. (And it is no small irony that, having constantly reminded himself of how soon he will be forgotten, he and his writings are still the focus of so much reflection and study.)

For Aurelius, the role of death in his meditative life is to force him to live in the present. Reminding himself of the contingency of the future and the shortness of his influence are ways of ensuring that he places his focus on living well now. We must be clear in what he means by living well now. It has something, but only something small, in common with a mode of approaching life that is often encapsulated in the phrase "live for today". Living for today often means enjoying oneself in the moment, treating oneself to whatever one likes at that particular time. Implicit in that phrase is the idea that there is no guarantee of the future, so that one has to focus on the present moment. Buy that new suit, eat that expensive meal, call in sick to work, since you don't know what the future brings. Or, in the words of certain ancient Romans (assuredly not Aurelius): eat, drink and be merry, for tomorrow we die.

Aurelius was no hedonist. The Stoic view is much more concerned with learning to live at peace with oneself and with doing good to others. When Aurelius exhorts himself to live in the present, it is to wrest himself from any expectations he might place on the future in order to concentrate on living how he ought to live. If the future cannot guarantee him material success or good reputation or even long remembrance, then it would be folly to concern himself with these things. All he can control is how he lives in the present. So what he ought to do is live as he should in the moment. Be at peace, treat others well, recognize who he is: these are the tasks that meditating on death will help him focus on.

There is much in Aurelius's idea of living in the present that responds to the concerns about death we have raised so far. If death is inevitable and uncertain, and if it forms no accomplishment, then one might well want to orient oneself towards the present. As Aurelius knows, the future offers us no guarantees. Moreover, death is not something to live for, since it brings no wholeness to our lives. Better then, it would seem, to live *in* the moment, if not necessarily *for* the moment. We need not be Stoics in deciding to live in the moment. We might decide to live differently. But however we decide to live, the lesson of death is that that living should focus on the present. The lesson of Aurelius, then, applied more broadly to death, is that we ought to live in the present without regard to the future, whose existence is uncertain.

This idea, while tempting, is not sufficient. It is not sufficient to our understanding of death and, as I shall shortly point out, it is not sufficient to Aurelius's understanding of life. It certainly is his official doctrine, but he lives differently from his official doctrine, which is, in a way, only half of the truth. But first, there is the insufficiency of living in the present relative to our understanding of death. Death, as we saw, is uncertain. It can come at any time. It might come tomorrow. But then again — and this is the other side of the coin — it might not come tomorrow. Any of us might live on for many years. Most of us will. The problem with living in the present is that this is to act as though there really is no future. It is not to treat death as though it is uncertain, but instead as though it is certain: it will come tomorrow.

We need to be careful here because it is easy to go wrong. It's not that the doctrine of living in the present *says* that death will come tomorrow: far from it. But living in the present is to treat life as though death will come tomorrow. The reason for this is that it completely eliminates concern for the future. One lives now, without regard for a future that is uncertain. But for a future to be uncertain means both that it might not be there and that it might be. To disregard the future is to disregard the second possibility. In that way, it is to act as though death will come tomorrow. If we are to live in accordance with our understanding of death, if we are to live the fragility of our lives, we must not only take into account that death might come tomorrow. We must also take into account that it might not.

And, in fact, this is what Aurelius does, although he does not say it to himself. He takes the project of becoming a Stoic as something that he must learn to do *over time*. He is not a Stoic; at least, that is what he tells himself. He would like to become one. He recognizes that he falls short. So he must work on becoming a Stoic. He must work on it now, to be sure. But he must keep on working until he becomes better at it. In short, becoming a good Stoic is a project for Aurelius, one that is ongoing and that requires a temporally extended commitment. There is, of course, an urgency to it. That urgency derives from the uncertainty of the future. He might not have more time to devote to making himself a better Stoic. But then again he might, and he probably needs that time in order to learn how to become more disciplined in his life.

One might argue here that this is a mistaken view of what Aurelius is trying to do. After all, isn't his project one of learning to be able to live in the present? Even though the project takes place over time, when and if he accomplishes it what he will be doing is living in the present rather than for any future. I don't think that that is an accurate characterization of what he is up to. It is his own view, to be sure. But it doesn't really reflect how he wants to live. For instance, as a Stoic he wants to promote the welfare of others and of the community. To promote the welfare of others must somehow take the future into account. For instance, if I were to want to promote your welfare it would make a difference if I knew you were going to die tomorrow. I would probably focus on different things from those I would focus on if I knew you had many years to live. How I treat you, then, if I seek to treat you well, depends on how I think about your future. If your death is uncertain (although inevitable), then my behaviour towards you will reflect that recognition. It is impossible to treat someone well without some view of what their future might look like or of what would promote their well-being given an uncertain future. Aurelius takes this into account in his behaviour, although it does not find its way into his philosophical reflections on his behaviour.

Aurelius's *Meditations*, then, and the life he seeks to live in accordance with them, is not exactly a living in the present. It is a living in the present and at the same time in an uncertain future. There is a tension in his thought; or, better, there is a tension between his thought and what his thought would lead him to do. This tension leads us to a deeper issue. Stoic doctrine emphasizes that one should only seek to control what one can actually control. One cannot control the way the world is; one can only control how one reacts to the world. This is the source of what people think of as stoical behaviour: behaviour that reacts calmly in the face of adversity. For Stoicism, one must never have expectations of what the world will offer. The world often disappoints. If you hang your expectations and hope on the world, you are setting yourself up for that disappointment. Moreover, you are turning control of your life over to the world. It is better to retain the control yourself. If you can't control what goes on in the world, then focus your energies on what you can control: how you live in that world; and, more specifically, how you react to the world's vicissitudes.

This is the source of Aurelius's emphasis on living in the present. The future is something one cannot control. One might have influence on future events, but that influence is uncertain. And, of course, one cannot control the past. It has already happened, and cannot be altered. One can only control one's present: who one is now, at this moment. To live in the present as Aurelius would like to is to seek to control who one is towards oneself and others in the only part of one's temporal existence that one can actually succeed in controlling. That is in conformity with Stoic doctrine.

The problem, I have argued, is that this is impossible, or at least it is impossible if one wants to be a Stoic. Perhaps it is possible if all one wants is to live *for* the moment. But that isn't what Stoics, or what most of the rest of us, are after. The problem here – and this is the deeper problem I just referred to – concerns control. What the Stoic wants, and what Aurelius's desire to live in the present reflects, is to control who one is and what one becomes. But if what I'm saying here is right, then that desire for control misses one of the aspects of death: the uncertainty of the future. Living solely in the present seeks to eliminate the future as being of any concern. In that sense, it sees the inevitability of death but tries to elude its uncertainty.

The uncertainty of death is two-sided. It means that one is not assured that one is going to have a future. It also means that one is not assured that one will not have a future. To live with the uncertainty of death is to embrace both of these aspects, not just one. Aurelius's project of living in the present embraces the first aspect to the neglect of the second. To live with the full recognition of death is to be able to grasp both sides of uncertainty at the same time. Aurelius has one side, but he neglects the other. How he wants to live does not neglect it. How he *thinks* he wants to live does.

Living in the present, then, is one side of the coin of living with death. Living with an uncertain future is the other. In order to live the fragility of life, one must be able to do both at the same time. It is a task filled with tension, but is perhaps not impossible. And, in any case, it is something one can do more or less. It is not a black and white matter: either one lives the fragility of life or one does not. We can work on it, make ourselves better at it, and therefore live in the face of death more fully than before.

In order to understand how this works, let's recall what the fragility of life is. It is the vulnerability of life to death at all moments of its existence. This vulnerability is at once the source of life's value and significance (as we saw in Chapter 2 on immortality) and the source of its precariousness (as we saw in Chapter 1). It is what gives our lives a sense of meaning and at the same time can give us a sense of meaninglessness. Living in the present captures something important about the fragility of life, but only one side of it. To live in the present is to recognize that the future may not be there, that death could come tomorrow, and therefore that one needs to inhabit the moment as fully as one can. One does not need to live in the present only as a Stoic. There are many ways of living in the present. The lesson I want to draw from Aurelius is not that if we live in the present we will necessarily become Stoics. It is, instead, that the uncertainty of the future does push us in the direction of living in the present. How one might live in the present is a task each of us must take up for ourselves. As we saw at the outset of this chapter, the fragility of life in the face of death does not give us specific guidelines regarding how to live. It only gives us a broad framework. Living in the present is part of that framework.

But it is only a part; the other part concerns living with, rather than neglecting, an uncertain future. It means immersing oneself in projects within the recognition that those projects are all vulnerable to death and that inevitably some of them will fall to death. Recall that one of the key characteristics of being human is having projects that extend themselves into the future. We live in the future just as we live in the present. Imagine trying to live without projects, without a career trajectory, or relationships or hobbies. These are central elements of a human life. In facing death and the fragility of life we cannot abandon our projects to live in the present. We must integrate them somehow. And, for our purposes right now, the question is one of how to think about that integration. We saw that Aurelius seemed to remain immersed in his projects, even as he thought he was trying to live solely in the present.

It might seem like a contradiction to try to live both towards the future in one's projects and at the same time live in the present. It sounds as though the idea would be both to live in the present and not to live in the present, and both at the same time. Put that way, it does sound impossible. But it does not need to be thought of this way. There is no contradiction between living in the present and at the same time being immersed in one's projects. One can live engaged *in* the present and yet also engaged *by* one's projects that extend into the future.

Here's an analogy that might capture the idea. When I drive a long distance with someone I like, I enjoy talking with them. I have a friend in philosophy that I have planned "road trips" to conferences with, in order to have time to talk in the car. Our talks are long, drawn-out affairs that range over politics, the environment, philosophy and the state of our lives. I look at the road, am aware of the traffic and consider how far there is to go. But I'm also very much with my friend. I am both in the present in my relationship and in the future in my driving. There is no contradiction here. My life, and all of our lives, have the capacity for both.

This analogy also teaches us something more. My relationship with my friend is something I project out into the future. We sometimes discuss plans for future cooperative work and, even when we don't, in the background of our conversations is the idea that our relationship is not likely to end with this car ride (unless I become so involved in the moment that I forget where the other cars are). I am both in the present and in the future with my friend. That duality is the temporal framework of our relationship.

If we think of living in the present as something that excludes any projecting into the future, then it seems impossible to live in the present and towards the future. But there is no reason to think that. As with my relationship with my friend, the two can be entwined; they are not exclusive. If this is so, then the question becomes one of how to live towards the future in the face of death. How do we take up our projects knowing that we have no control over our death, and that our death is inevitable and uncertain? How do we take up the challenge of living towards a future that may or may not yield us the time we need for our current projects?

The task is to live towards the future in its contingency. It is to engage in projects with the full recognition that some or all of them may be cut off by death. This might appear to be difficult, but we have an ally at our disposal. It is the present. We might put the point this way: we live towards the future in the present. We do not shy away from the fact that our future may be taken from us, and that sooner or later it will. This does not stop us from projecting into the future, because to stop that would be to abandon much of what makes us human. But we do not take up the future as if it were guaranteed to us. We do not take it for granted. Death assures us of this. All we can take for granted, as Aurelius saw, is the present. So we take up the future in the present. We live in the present and in an uncertain future, and we live both now.

How might this be done? Let me offer an example. This example should not be taken as a model. There is no model for living the present and the contingent future in the present. But an example might make the idea more concrete. In the course of writing this book I have thought much about death. The ideas that appear here have preoccupied me in a way that they often don't. After all, I don't like to dwell on death any more than most people. Perhaps the only other time I have thought about death in such an extended way is during the seminar on death I taught some years ago. So, as I have been writing this book, I have had to face the possibility that the book would not be completed. I have wondered about how to think about this book, given that it might never see the light of day. This possibility became a little more concrete last week. As I was nearing the end of the book, I went for a week to a rain forest in Costa Rica, knowing that there were certain dangers associated with such a trip. (I should confess, however, that I did not know that I would come across several vipers, and would be lucky to have a guide to point them out.) Given the themes of the book, the prospect of not finishing it was one I had to entertain.

How does this affect my relationship to writing the book? I cannot say, because it would not be true, that the writing of this book itself is entirely its own reward. The possibility, remote as it was, that I would not finish the manuscript was disappointing. But it was not a source of despair. That is an important distinction. In Chapter 1 we raised the possibility of despair in the face of death. The contingency of the future need not lead to despair. Why not? In my case, I can cite at least two reasons. First, I enjoy writing. Sitting down at the computer each day with ideas that seem worth thinking and writing about is meaningful to me. In that sense, I can live in the present with this book. Being taken up with ideas in the way I do when I write does not need a future. It is an Aurelian present (except for the fact that as I write I am also thinking about where the ideas are going to go and how I will pursue them in later parts of the book).

But it would be self-deception on my part to say that I had no more investment in this book than the writing of it every day. I also wanted the book to be completed, and eventually published. (As a philosopher, however, potential sales do not figure prominently in my thoughts about the future of my writings.) I project that future out when I write. But I know, particularly in the case of this book, that that future may not come to pass. That is the contingency I seek to live with, to come to terms with. It is a projecting out into the future of a task that may not come to fruition. It is to stay with that task at this moment, even in the face of its precariousness.

How well do I do this? More or less well. I am aware of what it is that I would like to do, just as Aurelius is aware of what it is he would like to do. There are people much better at it than I am, even if they have not gone through the philosophical process traced in this book. A couple of them are people I have had the good fortune to know. I am aware of what I would like to do, and I try. But that is where most of us live our lives, isn't it?

Another example: the jazz saxophonist John Coltrane died in 1967 before his forty-first birthday. More than forty years after that, jazz saxophonists still play under his shadow. Coltrane played with many of the jazz greats of his era such as Thelonious Monk and

Miles Davis before moving on to form his own quartet in 1960. With this quartet, and different iterations of it, he began to explore the limits of jazz music. He studied not only jazz but also Indian and Eastern music, and his own playing began to take on an increasingly spiritual orientation. His saxophone playing was once described as "sheets of sound". He would play cascades of notes that had a trance-like quality. I've seen a few grainy film clips of his playing in the mid-1960s and indeed he looks like a man possessed by his instrument and the sounds coming through it. Coltrane's playing was a searching, and he kept pushing the music, experimenting with it in ways that often sound discordant and that lost part of his audience. His drummer, Elvin Jones, described an incident in which Coltrane seemed to want to go beyond the saxophone itself and started thumping his chest on stage in an effort to produce other, deeper sounds.

The intensity of his music as well as the experiments he engaged in are often studied and imitated by younger players. But Coltrane was not only an experimenter. He was a rigorous practitioner, playing scales and riffs and combinations for hours every day. A fellow musician once witnessed Coltrane's excitement when he happened across a new set of scales for practice (I believe they were from Rachmaninoff, but memory is a bit elusive here), and asked to go into the bedroom so they could practice it right away. When he performed he was ready to experiment, because he mastered all the standard saxophone sounds and variations that had preceded him.

Although he certainly did not reflect on death, Coltrane's life was lived as one of fragility. Unlike many of us, this fragility was funnelled in a single direction: that of playing music. However, he approached his music in the way I suggest we might approach death. There is no doubt that, both onstage and off, he lived in the moment of his playing. He was absorbed by his instrument and the sounds that he brought out of it. No one who has seen him in concert or on tape doubts this. This absorption, however, did not mean that he could not orient his solos towards the future. Elvin Jones once commented that people who saw his playing mistook him for being lost in the music. On the contrary, Jones noted, although he was into his music he always seemed to know what he was doing and where he wanted to push it. This does not mean that he knew where it would wind up. But, even while in the moment, he was at the same time not entirely of the moment. Coltrane was at once absorbed, projecting and searching. Perhaps it is that unique combination that made him a spell that still hangs over contemporary jazz.

Most of us do not have the commitment to a single project that Coltrane did to his. This should not be surprising. Most of us are not destined to greatness. This does not mean, however, that we cannot in our own ways live both in the present and in the future. We are, except for a few among us, more scattered among different projects than Coltrane was – or than other great musicians, scientists and athletes are. But we can inhabit those projects both in the present in which we live and towards the future that we may or may not have before us. We can live our lives, pursue our careers, engage our friends and follow our passions, in both the fullness of the moment and the contingency of the future.

If we do so, particularly in the face of the recognition of death and the fragility of life, we are more likely to be sensitive to the distinction between the important and the petty in our lives. Death helps separate life's wheat from its chaff. It is not that each moment must be a sublime experience. To seek that would be to neglect the future for the sake of the present. Projects involve a commitment to the future, a commitment that almost always requires some degree of mundane work. Children must be driven to school. A political campaign needs to have envelopes stuffed and folded or leaflets handed out on street corners. Mastering a musical instrument requires much scale practice. In a love relationship, somebody has to go to the store or do the laundry or bring the car to the mechanic to have that grinding noise checked out. The face of death does not prevent these things. Instead it performs two other tasks. First, it asks of us which among our projects are the ones worth pursuing. What matters and what does not? It is easy, as we go through life, to pick up projects that add no significance to our lives or that remain with us solely out of habit. Recognizing the fact of one's death helps one sift through our projects in order to separate out those that contribute in some way to making us who we want to be.

The other task performed by the face of death is not *about* our projects but *within* them. This task is at least as important as the first one, and maybe more so, because it concerns temptations that we fall into too easily. My job is, of course, in academia. It is important to me. In the face of imminent death, I would quit it in a moment to be with those I love. That is to say, I would live solely in the present. But in the face of a death that is at once inevitable and uncertain, the projects my job involves are significant to my life. However, there are a number of things that crop up with this job that are not significant, and that a good look at death would allow me to walk away from or at least take a step back from. Those who are also in academia or in any large organization will readily know what I'm talking about here: office politics – who gets the corner office, who the boss likes and doesn't like, how exactly the flow chart of responsibilities is structured, who is getting undeserved perks or a few more dollars to travel, what authority each person gets to exercise and, just to add one peculiar to philosophy, who is doing real philosophy and who is just engaged in pointless critique or meaningless jargon. Every job has its politics, and many of us get tempted by it sooner or later. I would like to say that I'm always above it, but I'm not. And in most cases when I get caught up in it, I regret it after the battle wanes.

Death gives some perspective to all this. It poses the question: if you are going to die, you know not when, is this an element of your project you really must engage yourself in? There are, of course, micropolitical issues that matter. Sexism and racism, for instance, find their way into the workplace in the guise of office politics and should be confronted. But much of what passes for office politics is really of no account, and our engagement in it does not so much display our skill at navigating our work environment as it does our forgetting of ourselves as mortal creatures. Within our projects, then, as well as in regard to which projects we choose, the face of death helps us sort the significant from the insignificant, the aspects of our present and future that matter from those that don't.

All of this stems from the fragility of life. Knowing that we die, bearing our death in mind, we distinguish between what is impor-tant and what is not. We let go of projects that we have taken on for reasons that do not matter or no longer matter to us. Within the projects we embrace, we step aside from their petty moments. Instead, we concentrate on those aspects that are the reason we engage in those projects in the first place. Life, as we say, is too short. First, it is literally too short. It is always too short, even if immortality is too long. Secondly, it is too short to allow getting side-tracked into projects and squabbles and frustrations and temp-tations that aren't in the end significant.

The fragility of life tells us that it is death that at once threatens and gives meaning to our lives. Without death, I would have no reason to choose among the projects facing me. Office politics might not matter, but neither would I have any reason to avoid them. With death, I must choose. And in choosing, I must recog-nize that my choices may or may not be carried through. Now, when I am young and healthy, I am more likely to see those projects further along. My friendships, my career, my family rela-tionships, my writing: all of these are likely to see a future. They are not guaranteed; but nor are they eliminated from the outset. As I get older, the prospect of their elimination increases. But it is always there.

The fragility of life leads me, then, not to abandon my projects but to live them in their precarious character. I do not abandon my projects for the sake of solely living in the present. But nor do I abandon the present for projects that are always haunted by my death. I bring the two – present and future – together, the first in its existence and the second in its contingency. That is what it means to live in the face of death.

Death is the ultimate source of both the tragedy and the beauty of a human life. Moreover, death's tragedy is the source of life's beauty and vice versa. Although it is better that we are mortal, it is nevertheless a shame that we have to die. To die brings to a point-less end the involvements that make up our lives. And yet without that pointless end those involvements themselves might have no point. They would only be part of the endless passing show. They would be unable to touch us. That is to say, without the beauty of the moments that we are granted in this life, our death would be no tragedy; and without the tragedy of death, those moments would have no beauty. In this sense, as in the other senses we have discussed, death is the deepest and most important fact about us. To be human is to die and, more importantly, to know that one will die throughout one's life, even when (or especially when) we go to great lengths to avoid that knowledge.

Back in 2004, when I was on the plane that seemed to be heading for the Empire State Building, I was not living a philosophical reflection on death. But death was making my life clear to me. Had I not been mortal I would not have asked about my life. I would not have recognized that the life I had been living was the life I wanted to live, even if it didn't always seem that way. I would not have recognized that what I had fashioned, with the help of a lot of good fortune, was something that was, at least to me, worth having fashioned.

This recognition had another side, and it still does. I did not regret my life in those moments, but neither did I want it to end. I had come to terms with my life, but not to peace with my death.

The fact that I did not regret my life, even though it gave me solace in those moments, in the same gesture gave me more desire to continue. My life had been a good life; there was no reason for it to end then.

The goodness of my life until that moment in 2004 gives me no guarantee for the future. The future of any person is, as we have seen, contingent. Will events conspire so that the next time I face my possible death I form a different judgement from that day on the plane? I cannot say for sure. There are many things I cannot control about my future, my death being one of those. My hope is only that, in so far as my own contribution to my future is concerned, I can carry the lessons of my death close enough to me that I am not led astray in the time that remains.

For all of us, our death is difficult to face. It may not be the most difficult thing to face. The death or decline of a loved one, particularly one's child, may well be more difficult. Nevertheless, it is difficult. It is a difficulty that is defining for each of us as a human being. The argument of this book has been that if we understand this difficulty, if we are willing to face it squarely without illusion or escape, we might use its power to make something of ourselves that we do not regret. To forge our lives under the haunting shadow of death is both our reality and our opportunity. Death is what makes us the vulnerable creatures that we are and what gives us the tools to fashion that vulnerability into something worth having lived. The task for us, for each of us in the face of each of our deaths, is to live towards our end and with our end in a way, or in several ways, that casts a light within that darkness that ultimately engulfs us.

Further reading

As important as the theme of death is, it is surprising how marginal a theme it is in philosophical literature after the ancients. Perhaps no group of philosophers integrated death into their reflections more than what are called the Hellenistic philosophers: those who wrote after the classical period of Plato and Aristotle. In the Epicurean tradition, Epicurus's short summary of his work that has come to be called "Principal Doctrines" contains the arguments on death presented here. He also has arguments against death's being an evil in his letters to Herodotus and Menoeceus. These can be found in any collection of his writings. His later follower Lucretius incorporates his reflections on death in his long poem "On the Nature of Things", especially the third book. Marcus Aurelius's *Meditations* has reflections on death scattered throughout.

In Eastern philosophy, the Taoist philosopher Chuang Tzu has reflections on death sprinkled through the collection *Basic Writings* (1964). These reflections usually take the form of stories, which Chuang Tzu recounts with a gentle sense of irony.

Among contemporary philosophers, Thomas Nagel's essay "Death" (1970) is a profound reflection on death as an evil, as is Bernard Williams's essay "The Makropoulos Case" (1976), which is in part a response to Nagel's essay. Chapter 6 of Martha Nussbaum's *The Therapy of Desire* (1994) engages Lucretius, Nagel and Williams, and extends their reflections on death. In addition, the book itself is a sensitive treatment of Hellenistic philosophy.

Perhaps the most important sustained reflection on death is Part 1 of the Second Division of Heidegger's *Being and Time*, J. Stambaugh (trans.) (New York: SUNY Press, 1996). The themes regarding death outlined in Chapter 1 are drawn largely from that work.

In addition to the philosophical literature, there are a number of literary treatments of death. The most often discussed is probably Tolstoy's *The Death of Ivan Illyich*, L. Solotaroff (trans.) (New York: Bantam Books, 1981). The reason I did not discuss it here is only that other works helped me frame my issues better. However, I have certainly been influenced by Tolstoy's profound following of a man facing death.

Jorge Luis Borges's story "The Immortal", which I recounted at the beginning of Chapter 2, is from his collection *Labyrinths* (1962). Like so many of Borges's stories, it gives us much to think about. Another reflection on immortality that did not make an appearance here but is worth reading is Milan Kundera's *Immortality*, P. Kussi (trans.) (New York: HarperCollins, 1991), a novel much taken up with the question of what lives on and how people themselves seek to live on.

A contemporary novel that treats death with sensitivity and originality is Jim Crace's *Being Dead* (London: Viking, 1999). It alternates chapters of an old couple's lives with chapters detailing their physical decomposition after their murder. The juxtaposition forces a confrontation with death that turned out to be one of the starkest for the students in the seminar I taught on death.

References

Borges, J. L. 1962. "The Immortal". In his *Labyrinths*. New York: New Directions.

Chuang-Tzu 1964. *Basic Writings*, B. Watson (trans.). New York: Columbia University Press.

Epicurus 1994. *The Epicurus Reader: Selected Writings and Testimonia*, B. Inwood, L. P. Gerson (trans.). Indianapolis, IN: Hackett.

Marcus Aurelius 2006. *Meditations*. Harmondsworth: Penguin.

Nagel, T. 1991. "Death". In his *Mortal Questions*, 1–10. Cambridge: Cambridge University Press.

Nussbaum. M. 1994. *The Therapy of Desire*. Princeton, NJ: Princeton University Press.

Williams, B. 1976. "The Makropoulos Case: Reflections on the Tedium of Immortality". In his *Problems of the Self*, 82–100. Cambridge: Cambridge University Press.

Index

afterlife   12–21, 36–7, 53, 79–85,
        93
angst   40–41
Aurelius, Marcus   40, 85, 96–105,
        107–8
    Meditations   97–8, 103

Borges, Jorge Luis   45, 48, 53, 55,
        62, 66, 68, 73
    "The Immortal"   45–9, 62, 66,
        69
Buddhism   15–18, 23, 47, 81–2

Christianity   12–18, 81–2
Chuang Tzu   81–2
Coltrane, John   60, 108–10

Dewey, John   22

Epicurus   23–5, 29–31, 88
eternity   52–3

fragility of life   85, 93–6, 104–5,
        110, 112–13

Hadot, Pierre   97
Heidegger, Martin   9, 21–2, 25,
        34–5, 40
    Being and Time   21–2

Hinduism   16
Hume, David   50

immortality   3, 11, 42–3, 45–78,
        79, 83–95, 112
Islam   15–16

Jones, Elvin   109–10
Judaism   15–16

Lucretius   88–90, 92–3

Nagel, Thomas   31, 54, 65–6, 73,
        94
Nietzsche, Friedrich   37
Nussbaum, Martha   62–4, 73–6, 78

pain   23–5, 30–31, 38, 76–7
Pascal, Blaise   21
pleasure   23–5, 30–31

spiritual exercises   97–8
Stoicism   96–105
Swift, Jonathan   53–4

Taoism   18, 81–2, 90–93

Williams, Bernard   66, 68, 73–8,
        83, 92